THE PRACTICAL GUIDE TO THE UNITED STATES CONSTITUTION

THE PRACTICAL GUIDE TO THE UNITED STATES CONSTITUTION

A HISTORICALLY ACCURATE YET ENTERTAINING OWNERS' MANUAL FOR THE FOUNDING DOCUMENTS

TOM MCHALE

IPG PRESS

CONTENTS

1

AN OWNERS' MANUAL - FOR GOVERNMENT

"Small government is a threat to liberty!"

– James Madison (Paraphrased)

"Big government is a threat to liberty!"

– James Madison (Paraphrased)

How many words does it take to explain the United States Constitution? Eight.

Those baby kissers in Washington work for us.

There you have it; I hope you enjoyed the book!

But seriously, if you were to boil off the legalese and Byzantine terminology to make a constitutional reduction sauce, that's what you'd get. Sure, there's a little more detail in its 4,543 words plus the additional 7,591 in its 27 amendments. It defines the basic rules by which our government is supposed to play. It's intended to protect liberty and natural rights. It introduces supporting concepts like the separation of power. But, the simple idea remains that, as a people, we voluntarily consent to be governed by representatives of our choosing.

It's a delightfully selfish idea; we do this for our benefit. We're in charge of everything. All rights are ours. Sometimes, we elect to transfer some of our rights and authority back to the government so that society operates more efficiently. We'll get into that in plenty of detail later, so for now, digest that you and I, along with all our friends, family, and neighbors, are the big cheeses.

The Constitution is a big deal because it's the national owner's manual. Yet, as important as it is, 173.29 trillion people have never even read it. OK, so maybe that number is more of an estimate, but we're still fairly confident that most people know less about constitutional concepts than the composition of spackle.

Even among those who have read it, it remains largely misunderstood. The Constitution is just not all that exciting to read because it's peppered with obscure words like "attainder," "enumeration," and "emolument." So maybe the founders were vocabulary snobs. Cut them a break—you couldn't focus on simplicity either if you kept getting wig powder in your eyes.

Here's the great news. We will help avoid constitutional constipation by making it easy enough for a second grader to understand its meaning. No, wait. We can do better than that. We will make the Constitution so easy to understand that a six-term Congressman can get it. An impossible dream? Maybe, but this isn't just an adventure; it's our job.

Many modern social media scholars derisively refer to the Constitution as "that 200-year-old tree." Here's the thing. While early drafts of the Constitution were likely written on hemp paper, the founders placed inestimable value on the final product. That called for authentic parchment. Yes, some guy went behind the barn and skewered a sheep to make the paper. Ewww.

To fully appreciate the epic achievement that is the Constitution, you have to know something about the events leading to its creation.

That little revolutionary spat with the British wasn't a sudden thing—it took decades of all manner of bad behavior before people shouldered their muskets.

The unique circumstances leading up to the Revolutionary War presented an opportunity to rethink how people could govern themselves in a free and sustainable way. So, to understand the provisions in the Constitution, it's essential to know about the aspirations and concerns of the founders. We're going to start this book with an overview of the historical events leading up to the Constitutional Convention. Then we'll get into the contents of our national rule book.

Even after the decision had been made to whip up our set of operating instructions, there was little smooth sailing. If you think today's political discourse manners are at an all-time low, you should have seen the feathers fly during the design process. Remember the last time you attended a homeowners' association or PTA meeting? Stop and think about the angst, pettiness, infighting, alliances, fist fights, and political struggles. Got a clear mental picture? Good. Now multiply that by eleventy-nine trillion, and you have a good idea of the process of designing and implementing the Constitution. It was a remarkable achievement.

The, let's say, "vigorous" debate was part of what made the birth of a new nation under a constitutional republic framework such an incredible accomplishment. In the founders' view, all of that disagreement was just fine. They felt monumental decisions should be argued, debated, attacked, and defended. You might think of the process as a form of "policy smelting." Apply enough heat, rigor, and torture to the process, and something good will come out, even if a few wigs caught fire in the process.

The bottom line is this. Politics ain't easy and never has been, partly because it establishes power. And right behind a fine steak dinner and burying our noses in smartphones, the pursuit of power and influence is right at the top of our collective priority list.

With that said, here goes...

Politicians have been kissing babies forever. Why? Who knows? But not all seeking office pretend to adore random children. According to legend, the seventh President of the United States, Andrew Jackson, flat-out refused to smooch strange munchkins. When handed a child on the campaign trail, he reportedly shuffled the kid off to his Secretary of War. Maybe he thought the kid was officer material? Richard Nixon also poo-pooed the practice, stating that stunts like that would "make him look like a jerk."

2

A BRIEF PRE-CONSTITUTIONAL HISTORY

"THROOP, PENNSYLVANIA OR BUST!"

– Early American Settlers

To understand the significance and intended meaning of four pages of dried-out sheepskin, you must understand the trials and tribulations of all the folks who packed a few things in their satchels and headed to the new land soon to become the United States.

Soon after the calendar turned 1600 AD, there was a tremendous influx of settlers looking for a new way of life. People arrived not just from Great Britain but also Spain, France and other European countries. The Spanish headed towards what's now known as Florida, while the French pursued interests in the area presently occupied by the state of Louisiana. The English focused on the coastal states, edging inland. The land was characterized by a baker's dozen new colonies with competing and often changing interests. Before long, this new frontier was home to a couple of million Europeans of mixed heritage.

The first United States Census took place in 1790, as outlined in Article I, Section 2 of the Constitution. The results? By that time, there were 3,929,214 people in the United States.

Escalation of Authoritarian Rule

Things weren't easy in the new territories, and disputes over the usual topics created unusual and sometimes shifting alliances. Not surprisingly, the English and French were often at odds. The Seven Years War began in 1754. No, it wasn't over a long-standing dispute over whether it's OK to put accent marks over various letters and who made the best boudin noir.

The Seven Years War resolved the ownership of a vast tract of land stretching from Newfoundland to Baton Rouge, which the French called "New France." For incomprehensible reasons, when the English took over this property after the war, they sidestepped the obvious name of "New England and referred to their new real estate as "the land west of the Appalachians."

Here's why this deal became, well, a big deal to the soon-to-emerge United States. King George immediately banned the development and colonization of all of this new property, essentially claiming it for himself, with The Royal Proclamation of 1763. To the adventurous folks who risked all to build new lives, not having access to all of this land was a slap in the face. Strike one against the King.

The eternal bad blood between the English and French played an essential role in the outcome of the American Revolution, but that's a different story. What was important at this point was that colonists had shifting loyalties. The French had just lost a war and a bunch of property. The colonists, under England, had, in theory, gained it. However, the Royal Proclamation of 1763 took it back off the table. As a result, the colonists and the French now shared frustration with King George.

When the French were present in force and vying for some affection from British colonists, England had to put on the appearance of behaving. Once the French were driven out, England took a more hard-nosed approach to governing the new colonies.

The Royal Proclamation of 1763, issued by the Crown, was more about wheeling and dealing with the Native American population at the time than penalizing the colonists. After dealing with a revolt by Chief Pontiac, King George declared the land west of the Appalachian Divide off limits to give the Indians some peace, avoid fighting yet another war, and negate the need to provide security to hordes of settlers heading west.

So, the English had just won a costly war and needed money to restock the royal treasury. The solution was acting, not the Hollywood type, but rather tax and policy acts that imposed an additional economic burden on the colonists.

In April 1764, George III's Parliament passed the Sugar Act. While it doesn't sound like much now, the three-penny tax on molasses was a big enough deal to drive early colonial merchants into hardship. Parliament passed an expansion of the Currency Act later that year. While New England had been banned from issuing its own paper currency since 1751, the new act dramatically expanded this restriction and required colonial businesses to ship their legal currency back to England to pay creditors. As a result, there just weren't many bills to go around—literally.

The Stamp Act of 1765 was yet another legislative burden. Virtually every type of paper product had to have an embossed tax stamp, meaning that King George got a piece of the action, whatever it was. As if taxing paper wasn't bad enough, this was the first time the King imposed a tax on business "within the colonies" rather than just taxing international trade.

Needless to say, people were mighty ticked off. One night in August 1765, an angry mob of Stamp Act protesters crashed a dinner party hosted by Massachusetts Lieutenant Governor and Chief Justice Thomas Hutchinson. The governor and his guest barely escaped before the ill-tempered crowd polished off what was left of a very lovely claret.

The following day, the colonists took drastic measures and created the Stamp Act Congress. You know things are bad when people think a new Congress will improve the situation. This Stamp Act group convened in New York to draft "a very stern letter" to King George. This communique asked George not to tax them without local consent. The colonists had a valid argument, for as English citizens, they had a right to their own local representation. The complaints fell on deaf ears, and more taxes came rolling in, as they always do.

You might expect an exciting factoid here related to the Sugar or Stamp taxes, but you'd be wrong. Instead, we're going to talk about George Washington's wooden teeth. They weren't really made of wood—that would be ridiculous. They were made of ivory, bone, lead, copper wire, and recovered human and animal teeth.

Through the rest of 1765, frustration grew among the locals as all these taxes cut into their personal and business dealings. By 1766, shocked by the level of general outrage, Parliament got its act together and killed the acts. Not able to admit defeat to the Colonists, Parliament added a clause to this decision, essentially saying that they were "in charge" and "looking out for the interests of the colonies." Hence, there was no need for local representation. Later, this turned out to be kind of a big deal.

By 1767, Parliament had drifted out of touch with the Colonists once again and issued a new batch of taxes on British imports to the colonies. In response, the Colonists increased local production and implemented boycotts to decrease dependence on British imports.

Lest you think all this angst only generated idle threats, things got serious in 1770. In early March, a group of Bostonians pelted a garrison of Redcoats with snowballs. A brawl ensued, and the British shot and killed five of the protesters. For obvious reasons, this event became known as the Boston Massacre.

In 1773, George III dreamed up an early form of a corporate bailout. At the time, the British East India Company was in serious trouble. They'd bought way too much tea and couldn't sell it. King

George and Parliament decided that the British East India Company was too big to fail and hatched a plan to unload the excess tea on the colonists.

In a move that could only be dreamed up by politicians and communicated with a straight face by a White House Press Secretary, the British East India Company tried to dump tea way below market price, but with a tax attached. The idea was to drive the local caffeine distributors out of business and lock up the market in favor of the Crown.

You already know the result. Frustrated colonists dumped crates of Earl Grey into Boston Harbor as a protest. Once again, frustration transitioned from verbal and written protest to physical.

Not everyone was all excited about the Boston Tea Party. Many patriots, including the most patriot-est of them all—George Washington—weren't keen on the destruction of personal property. As we'll see throughout this book, personal property was a big deal and part of one's natural rights, so the destruction of another's property, even if they were acting like weenies, was frowned upon.

In response to the growing unrest and the Boston Tea Party, the powdered wigs in Parliament became upset and flexed their muscles. Parliament was sick and tired of not being respected by the Colonists, while the Colonists were sick and tired of being bossed around by people 3,269 miles away who were a crumpet short of afternoon tea.

The very first thing the British did was close Boston Harbor, which now had the distinct aroma of stale tea anyway. No harbor meant no business. No more shipping, no more lucrative exports to foreign countries, and no more much-needed imports. The closing of the port was no small matter, and the intent was clearly punitive against the people of Massachusetts. King George insisted that the harbor would remain closed until tea partiers forked over payment for damages and rebellious behavior ceased.

As punishment, Parliament enacted the Massachusetts Government Act. This decree effectively ended any semblance of local authority by placing the Governor, Parliament, and the King in charge of all government hiring. In business terms, the move was a hostile takeover, and the Americans thought the whole idea a pile of codswallop.

The Administration of Justice Act gave royal officials in America, at least in the Colonists' view, the ability to commit beastly crimes without consequence. The act empowered the Governor to move trials of British officials accused of wrongdoing to England or elsewhere in the empire at his discretion if he felt that a fair trial could not be had locally. Certainly, local witnesses were free to travel to London to testify if they were willing to sail six to twelve weeks, each way, at their expense, taking off work for the duration. For obvious reasons, the Administration of Justice Act brassed off the Colonists to no end.

Another punitive action, the Quartering Act, decreed that the colonies would be required to house British soldiers, if needed, in unoccupied buildings. While not a big deal practically speaking, this act nonetheless threw a little extra gas on the growing dumpster fire, which was now stoked up to the boiling point on the revolution thermometer.

As usual, this whole kerfuffle was not so much about the specifics of all of these acts but the whole idea of being bossed around in general. As British citizens, the Colonists were accustomed to having natural or pre-existing rights to things like representation and freedom. The more the Colonists asserted the independence they believed they already had, the more the crown cracked down on them.

And that festering, bubbling cauldron of resentment leads us to... The First Continental Congress, the Second Continental Congress, and the Declaration of Independence. These gatherings and their outputs developed many of the fundamental principles which would soon be included in the United States Constitution.

Speaking of "acting," the theater business was in full swing at the time of the Revolution. The Dock Street Theater opened in downtown Charleston, South Carolina way back in 1736 and others followed throughout the colonies. Predictably, early theater focused on classics like Othello and

Hamlet, but we can't find any surviving patrons to tell us if the acting was intolerable or not.

The First Continental Congress

The Americans organized the First Continental Congress in September 1774. The goal was to coordinate a protest on behalf of all the colonies against King George's oppressive attitude. While George's spiteful acting was aimed at the colony of Massachusetts, the other colonies figured, probably correctly, that they were next in line for a double-helping of torment and beastly manners. In their view, King George and his cronies in Parliament had gone completely off their trolley.

The decision to call a Congress was in direct response to the unbearable, unendurable, insufferable acts. The goal was to find a way to get the brutish monarch to lighten up. Twelve of the 13 Colonies sent delegates to Philadelphia in September and October 1774. Only Georgia declined the invitation because they needed British help fighting off Native Americans and didn't want to tell the Brits to get stuffed just yet. Everyone has their price.

Even though there was plenty of anger to go around, things moved at a snail's pace. Perhaps the Congress took so long to produce results due to differences of opinion on how to handle the Brits. Conservatives like John Jay and South Carolina's own Edward Rutledge wanted to send a message, but nothing too bold. Radicals led by Samuel Adams wanted to take a more aggressive stance.

The result of this first Congress was about the same as the result of any other Congress—not much. The most tangible outcome from the Congress was a boycott of English goods. Most delegates wanted to restore proper relations with the Crown after finding a resolution to the coercive acting situation and believed that a boycott was an excellent way to express displeasure without stepping too far over the line towards outright revolution.

After about seven weeks of debate and posturing, the delegates also whipped up another stern letter to King George asking him to stop being such a plonker.

Interestingly, the petition to the king got buried in the usual deluge of paperwork in both the House of Lords and the House of Commons. As a result, it never got any attention, and it's unclear whether King George ever even saw it.

Oh, and like most other Congresses, this one finished with a resolution to have another in the future if more bloviating and posturing were required.

When the Japanese bombed Pearl Harbor, the original Constitution was moved from Washington, DC, to Fort Knox for safekeeping.

Shots Fired!

Just a few months after the First Continental Congress, things went pear-shaped. The embargo implemented by the First Congress succeeded in reducing imports from Britain by over 90 percent. It might have brought about some policy change, but no matter, war was in the wind.

The tensions that had been building for years erupted into a full-blown shooting war on April 19, 1775. By then, Parliament had briefed the King that they considered the colonies in a state of open revolt and that serious action was required.

In a move designed to be secret and preemptive, the British Army planned to raid and destroy suspected weapons stockpiles in the towns of Lexington and Concord just outside British-controlled Boston. Word got out, however, and the colonists were able to stash their war gear elsewhere and mount a hasty defense. In part, the early warning resulted from Paul Revere's desperate midnight ride, during which he and William Dawes provided a crucial heads up to the militia along the way.

By the time the British arrived in Lexington, about 80 local militiamen had assembled under the leadership of one Captain Parker. Remember, there was no war going on—yet—and the Declaration of Independence was still over a year in the future. By most accounts, Parker intended to defend against any outrageous British behavior and show a little manliness, so his militia did not attempt to stop the British regulars. According to one participant, Parker said something to the effect of "Stand your ground; don't fire unless fired upon, but if they mean to have a war, let it begin here." You have to admit, Parker exceeded expectations in the creative manliness category.

To make a long story short, tensions ran high, and somebody shot at somebody else. No one knows for sure who started it, but the tense standoff turned into a street fight resulting in one British wounded, eight militiamen killed, and another ten wounded. Some believe this was the "shot heard around the world," but not Ralph Waldo Emerson. Stay tuned for a hot second, and we'll tell you why a few pages from now.

The British continued to Concord to complete their mission of finding and destroying militia supplies. As British troops approached Concord, Colonel James Barrett moved his force to a ridge overlooking the town. Not looking to start a ruckus prematurely, the militiamen allowed the British to complete their search of the area. As the war supplies had been moved long before the British arrived, this search was uneventful. As the morning unfolded, Barrett moved his men closer to the North Bridge, where once again, a shot rang out, starting another skirmish. The British forces were divided at this point, so the Colonials outnumbered the Redcoats near the North Bridge by about 400 to 90. After a few volleys of fire, the Americans drove away the British, who retreated to regroup with the remainder of their forces in the area.

After completing their search of Concord, the British began the long march back to Lexington and Boston. Throughout the morning, militias from surrounding areas had joined the fight, and the American forces now numbered over 2,000. In a brilliant battlefield tactic, the Americans leapfrogged the retreating British troops all the way back, inflicting many casualties. By the time the British made it back to Boston, an estimated 15,000 militia members from all over New England had joined in the fight and surrounded the British stronghold of Boston proper.

And that's how a full-blown war began with a single musket shot on Lexington Common. Strangely enough, the war for independence had begun, yet the colonists had yet to declare independence formally.

Did you know that the guy famous for his midnight ride warning that the British were coming was into heavy metal? Paul Revere was an accomplished silversmith and an engraver by trade. Less commonly known is his leap from simple craftsman to industrialist. After the Revolutionary War, he focused on volume production methods and became one of the country's leading bell casters. Hundreds of Paul Revere and Sons bells ended up in churches and other buildings across the country. The company also cast cannons and parts for shipbuilding.

The Second Continental Congress

Just a couple of months after the shooting started, Congress reconvened. After all, if you're going to be at war with a major world power, you ought to at least form committees. The first action of the Second Continental Congress was to create an army. The second move of the Second Congress was to designate a commanding General—George Washington—who agreed to take the job under the condition that he not be paid. Yes, those were the days when "service" was a meaningful part of "public service."

Anyway, besides managing the war, four items of import, at least in the context of this book, were resolved by the Second Continental Congress: The Declaration of the Causes and Necessity of Taking Up Arms, the Olive Branch Petition, the Declaration of Independence, and the Articles of Confederation. Oh, and Georgia got its act together in July 1775 and sent official delegates to this Congress, so all 13 colonies were represented.

In summary, the Second Continental Congress assumed the role of a national governing body. They created a currency and a post office for the United Colonies, although all participants were clear that the real power still resided in the states.

Ever wonder who signed these important documents first? There must have been some reluctance to be the first to sign the Declaration of Inde-

pendence. After all, those guys were quite literally signing their death warrants. Most believe that as President of the Congress, John Hancock was the first to pick up the quill for that one. Maybe that would explain his signature's elegant and sweeping style as a hint to the others. "Be neat! This is important!" As for the Constitution, details are sketchy. Most believe that George Washington signed first because of the respect he commanded and the fact that he was President of the Constitutional Convention.

The Olive Branch Petition

The Congress approved the Olive Branch Petition on July 5, 1775. Members of the Second Congress were divided on just how far to push for independence as opposed to reconciliation with Britain through agreement on trade, tax, and representation issues.

The primary author of the Olive Branch Petition, John Dickinson, was clearly in the reconciliation camp. Some on the other side, John Adams, for one, felt that war for total independence was inevitable but were willing to let things play out before pushing too hard for complete separation.

While this petition communicated a desire for agreement, reconciliation, and continued loyalty to the crown, its sincerity was questionable. The shooting had already started, and the English were royally ticked. Just one day later, on July 6, 1775, the Second Congress approved the Declaration of the Causes and Necessity of Taking Up Arms. It's hard to believe that anyone put much faith in a positive outcome from the Olive Branch Petition.

However, it did serve an essential purpose. In writing, the rebel government had expressed a "sincere" desire to reconcile with England. Now, when King George III rejected this plan, as everyone knew he would, the Americans would be united in the quest for total independence since the English would have scoffed at the proffered olive branch.

The phrase "the shot heard around the world" comes from Ralph Waldo Emerson's Concord Hymn. It refers to the shot fired at the North Bridge in

Concord, but it wasn't the first shot of the war. Earlier in the day, fire erupted at Lexington and from accounts of the North Bridge skirmish, a British soldier started the shooting inadvertently. Regardless, the militia's response may have represented the first shots of the Revolutionary War fired under orders.

The Declaration of the Causes

Even a literary and penmanship star like Thomas Jefferson needed a practice run to create the Declaration of Independence, and the Declaration of the Causes and Necessity of Taking Up Arms was it. While John Dickinson (yes, of Dickinson College) wrote the final draft of this document, it was Jefferson who did the early work. In case you were wondering, Dickinson also wrote the first stern letter to George III, so he was rapidly building a "troublemaker" reputation across the pond.

Regardless of Dickinson's penmanship skills, this Declaration of Causes was vital because it outlined why the Colonists were at war with the world's primary superpower. In a sense, this document was similar to a letter you might write your cable company after months and months of customer service problems. First, you rehash everything they did wrong and how their service failed. Then you talk about the valiant efforts you made to help them help you. Next, you go on and on about how patient you've been. Finally, you close with a threat to switch to satellite TV unless they get their act together. The Declaration of Causes and Necessity of Taking Up Arms was much the same but with hardly any four-letter words.

While a threat to switch to a much friendlier government was hard to miss, the closing language of the Declaration still proposed an amicable solution.

"Lest this declaration should disquiet the minds of our friends and fellow-subjects in any part of the Empire, we assure them that we mean not to dissolve that union which has so long and so happily subsisted between us and which we sincerely wish to see restored. Necessity has not yet driven us into that desperate

measure or induced us to excite any other nation to war against them. We have not raised armies with ambitious designs of separating from Great Britain and establishing independent states."

But no matter. In August 1775, King George issued a Royal Proclamation stating that the American colonists were "engaged in open and avowed rebellion."

Was the Declaration of the Causes and Necessity of Taking Up Arms a passive-aggressive statement or a sincere attempt to avoid war? Consider these excerpts from the original text.

"Our cause is just. Our union is perfect. Our internal resources are great, and, if necessary, foreign assistance is undoubtedly attainable."

"We shall lay them down when hostilities shall cease on the part of the aggressors, and all danger of their being renewed shall be removed, and not before."

Declaring Independence

As this de facto government started to discuss issues of national importance, like whether to become an independent nation, it became clear that they didn't yet have a country. How do you do things like sign treaties, send delegations to distant nations, and choose the official national bird without first creating a real government?

Many delegates didn't believe they had the authority to vote on whether to declare independence. Consequently, one of the early orders of business was to encourage the states to form their own revolutionary state governments so they could grant authority to the revolutionary state delegates to vote for revolution at the national level.

As June 1776 drew near, the calls for complete independence were clear, and the Second Congress was working on resolutions to sever ties with England. Concurrently, the delegates were evaluating ways to structure this loose coalition of 13 states, but we'll get to details on that in the next section.

On June 2, Richard Henry Lee of Virginia proposed the following resolution.

> "That these United Colonies are, and of right ought to be, free and independent States, that they are absolved from all allegiance to the British Crown, and that all political connection between them and the State of Great Britain is, and ought to be, totally dissolved."

There was still disagreement about whether this was the right time to sever ties with England, and a majority voted to recess for three weeks. As the assumption was that an independence vote would become unanimous, five delegates (John Adams, Roger Sherman, Benjamin Franklin, Robert R. Livingston, and Thomas Jefferson) were chosen to draft a formal declaration for public view.

During the congressional recess, Jefferson holed up in a second-story rental property on the outskirts of Philadelphia to write the first draft. After making some edits based on feedback from Adams and Franklin, Jefferson sent the draft to the committee of five and then to the entire Congress on June 28.

On July 2, 1776, the Second Continental Congress resolved to declare independence from Jolly Old England, with 12 of 13 colonies supporting the measure. New York abstained from that vote.

For two days, Jefferson's masterpiece was subjected to editing and criticism by a committee, and you know how smoothly committees perform tasks like jointly authoring a document. Two sections, each of which was a big deal to Jefferson, were struck from the document. One was a complaint against the British people for allowing their King to become such a tyrannical weenie. The other was a blistering condemnation of slavery and the British slave trade, which was still active at the time. Yes, there was much more to Thomas Jefferson than meets the eye. More on that later.

On July 4, 1776, the Declaration of Independence was approved, and Thomas Jefferson finally got a weekend off to enjoy doing anything but writing.

"The Second Day of July 1776 will be the most memorable Epocha in the History of America."

OK, so John Adams miscalculated when the rest of us would want to drink beer and play with pyrotechnics, but at least he was close.

The Rest of the Revolution

Since this book is about the United States Constitution and not the Revolutionary War, we'll summarize in the interest of brevity.

The Colonists got all cheeky and started a war. They won.

And while we kinda hate to admit it, the French helped quite a bit. Maybe for that reason, hostilities officially concluded with the Treaty of Paris in September 1783. Actually, the war had ended about a year earlier, but apparently, no one was in a big hurry to go to France to sign the papers, free beignets or not.

Now that the war was over, the really big fight began: the construction of a country.

Everyone knows the story of the original Thanksgiving holiday. Back in 1621, the Pilgrim settlers shared a meal of thanks with members of the Wampanoag tribe. What's not so well known is that the event that inspires fear among countless turkeys didn't become an annual thing until President Abraham Lincoln started that ball rolling during the Civil War. However, in 1789, George Washington declared November 26 as a National Day of Thanks. That was a Thursday, so perhaps that provided the inspiration for the timing of the annual Thanksgiving holiday.

Why the History Matters

We dedicated space in the book to review the history because the circumstances leading up to the revolution profoundly impacted the design and thinking behind the Constitution. Only by knowing the background of the struggle for self-governance does the theory behind the Constitution make sense.

As we'll see, the whole concept of the Constitution protects, not grants, inherent natural rights with which we're all born. It's kind of like that birthmark on your left foot. It's yours, and no one can take it away from you without your voluntary consent or by force, which would really hurt.

The whole design of our current government is one of mutual consent. No person or government has the "right" to rule over us. That's exactly what the colonists fought and died for during the American Revolution. They were sick and tired of what they perceived as oppression from a non-consent-based government. For the benefit of society as a whole, we willingly submit to the authority of a government of our choosing, at least until that government no longer represents our interests.

Next, let's explore those important concepts in more detail.

Alexander Hamilton got started with his influential political career at a young age. At just 19, he penned an essay titled "The Farmer Refuted," where he spoke to the purpose of legitimate government. In Hamilton's words, consent is an obligatory requirement of government.

"...for what original title can any man or set of men have, to govern others, except their own consent?"

3

A NEW TYPE OF GOVERNMENT

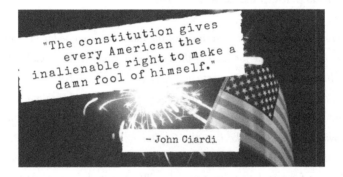

"The constitution gives every American the inalienable right to make a damn fool of himself."

– John Ciardi

Governing Theory

In the founders' view, government exists for one reason only: to subpoena and investigate each other. Just kidding! This is the real reason:

> To protect the natural rights of those who elect to be
> governed.

That's it.

Kind of like the phrase, "I'm pregnant," there's a lot more going on behind the scenes than those few words might imply. We'll get a lot deeper into the definition of natural rights and the whole concept of voluntarily submitting rights to be governed. For now, know the founding of the United States was a novel and difficult thing.

Never before had a nation designed itself, from the ground up, under the guiding principles that man is born with inalienable, God-given, natural rights, that he can self-govern, and that he can voluntarily surrender certain individual rights to a government created solely to protect them. The 40th President of the United States summed things up pretty well...

> *"We the people declared that the government is created by the*
> *people for their own convenience."*

This new system of government relies on some pretty amazing but obvious principles. Let's take a look.

There were fourteen original copies of the Bill of Rights, one for the federal government and one for each of the 13 original colonies. Only eight states still have their copies: Connecticut, Massachusetts, New Hampshire, New Jersey, Rhode Island, North Carolina, South Carolina and Virginia. One of those only recently reclaimed theirs. At the end of the Civil War, one of Sherman's soldiers broke into the Capitol Building and stole the North Carolina copy. He took it home to Ohio and later sold it to a local grain salesman for five dollars. In 2003, the FBI recovered the copy in a sting operation when a collector tried to sell it to the National Constitution Center for four million dollars. By 2007, after some fancy legal maneuvers, it was returned to North Carolina.

What Are Rights, Really?

If this new government's purpose is to "protect rights," it's essential to establish a baseline understanding of what rights are. Listening to politicians, it seems that we have all sorts of "rights" today. The right to life, the right to own things, the right to freely express ourselves, the right to healthcare, the right to have certain things paid for by the government, the right to housing and a good job, the right to leisure time, the right not to be offended, and apparently, the right to text while driving. Whether deep-fried butter at the State Fair is a natural right or just culinary suicide is still up for debate.

Over the past century, we've overseen an epidemic of "rights inflation." Knowing what rights are and, more importantly, what they're not, is crucial to understanding what the Constitution is all about. When the guys with wigs were arguing about how to best structure our fledgling government, they spent a lot of time and energy nailing down the true meaning of natural rights.

When considering the concept of natural rights in the founding sense, it's always important to do a rights check of everyone in the room to make sure that what's labeled a "natural right" is pure. What do we mean by pure? A natural right impacts you but cannot negatively impact the rights of others. Hold that thought for a hot second...

The Declaration of Independence enumerates "Life, Liberty, and the Pursuit of Happiness." So, to start with the third, we all have the right to the "pursuit of happiness."

As we'll discover throughout our look at the founding documents, definitions of various words are often slightly different from what we assume today. At the time that the Declaration of Independence was written, the term "happiness" was less about the feeling you get after scoring front row seats to a Milli Vanilli reunion concert and more about satisfaction resulting from your productive contributions to society. Other interpretations describe the 1776 meaning of the word as similar to "prosperity" or perhaps "well-being."

We won't get into the etymology debate here, mainly because "etymology" is a big word. Just know we're going to run across terms, like "happiness," which might have different meanings now than 200 years ago. For now, realize that the right to the pursuit of happiness can be stated as the right to pursue and accomplish your own well-being.

Getting back to the point, we all have a natural right to pursue happiness, prosperity, self-satisfaction, or whatever you want to call it. And we have this right forever, regardless of what any government says about it, right up to the point where our desire for "happiness" infringes on the rights of another.

Let's consider an example. Suppose my well-being relies entirely on scoring those Milli Vanilli tickets. Forget life, the ability to earn and acquire property and all the rest; I need those seats to realize my personal nirvana. That's just fine according to the concept of natural rights.

To be clear, it's up to me to figure out how to acquire those tickets. I can earn money to buy them or perhaps embark on a mega-fan campaign to get free backstage passes. The key is that it's my problem to figure out how to acquire them and no one else's. My right to pursue happiness doesn't in any way, shape, or form imply that a cheesy lip-syncing concert experience is owed to me. Others have no obligation to help me achieve the realization of this right. The government has no responsibility to ensure my happiness by subsidizing my Ticketmaster account. And I certainly can't steal or otherwise illicitly acquire the seats. Why not? Because that would be illegal, but more importantly, in the context of this discussion, it would be infringing on the right of whoever possessed those tickets in the first place. Even though they were unabashed frauds, the Milli Vanilli guys own those seats, so the rights to transfer them to someone else are theirs alone.

While it's a silly example, this type of "rights inflation" happens every day. It sounds great to have the "right" to food, healthcare, housing, vacation, or free Brown Sugar & Cinnamon Pop Tarts, but if that "right" is provided by forcibly taking money from others and therefore violating their property rights, it's not truly a natural right. The same concept applies to life and liberty. If my existence or freedom depends on infringing on another's natural rights, then ix-nay on the whole "rights" thing.

This idea of infringing on the right of another to claim your own rights has a flip side. As a free society, we as citizens have a duty and responsibility not to intrude on the natural rights of others. I have a duty not to steal or forge Milli Vanilli reunion tickets. We all have a duty not to harm others. We have a duty not to forcibly impose our will on others, thereby violating their right to freedom.

Keep in mind we're sticking to a purist definition of natural rights here because the concept is critical to understanding the meaning of the Constitution. The founders would (and did, according to their writings) take a hard line on the definition of an authentic natural right. That's not to say they were opposed to things that may benefit society, like caring for those experiencing hard times; they just felt that those types of compassionate activities ought to be done voluntarily (mostly) without forcing others to pay for them involuntarily. If someone is being "forced" to exhibit compassion, that's not all that compassionate, is it?

You might say the founders saw that rights couldn't be a zero-sum game. If I have a right, it can't, by definition, take away or reduce your rights. You might think of true rights as little individual bubbles. We have control over our own bubble of rights, but we can't pop someone else's.

Here's another quick bit of trivia. Did you know the Constitution is bilingual? If you look closely, you'll find it's written in two languages.

Which ones? English and Latin. Granted, the use of Latin is limited, including the phrases habeas corpus, pro tempore, and ex-post facto. Well, it's something.

I Consent to That

The interesting thing about freedom, at least in the context of the great American experiment, is that it requires submission to the government. Using the words "freedom" and "government" in the same sentence sounds silly when you think about it, kind of like having a "Best Gefilte Fish" category in the MTV Music Video Awards. If you were truly free, then how could you possibly be governed?

You don't have to read very far into the "Unanimous Declaration of the Thirteen United States of America," commonly known as the Declaration of Independence, to get a handle on how that apparent contradiction in terms works. Right near the beginning of the second paragraph, there's an explanation.

*"...they are endowed by their Creator with certain unalienable Rights, that among these are Life, Liberty and the pursuit of Happiness.—That to secure these rights, Governments are instituted among Men, deriving their just powers **from the consent of the governed**...."*

George Washington offered the following observation in a letter to the President of Congress dated September 17, 1787. *"Individuals entering into society must give up a share of liberty to preserve the rest."*

Let's break that down into an analogy that even a six-term congressman can understand.

As a free person, you can expect, under the concept of natural rights, that you have the right to keep and maintain your possessions. If a Capitol Hill lobbyist steals your brand new fidget spinner, your rights have been violated—forcibly in this case. With no government in place, your response might be to lock said offender up in jail for a period not to exceed 18 decades while withholding their afternoon nap privileges. Yeah, I know, that's a steep penalty. But they were a Capitol Hill lobbyist, and that's a primary offense on its own!

Technically, it's your right to protect your property from theft. Logistically, as much as you might want to, it makes little sense to build and staff a prison for just one offensive lobbyist, even though he stole something of incalculable value. On the other hand, if you and I and a few million of our friends elect to establish a government for the sole purpose of protecting our natural rights, then the concept of having the government run and staff a penitentiary for fidget spinner stealing trolls makes much more sense.

Here, you've voluntarily given up your right to apprehending and punishing fidget spinner thieves and transferred that power to the government. It's for the good of all of us to have a standardized way of dealing with dastardly gadget thieves, right? The idea is that the government we just created, voluntarily, can do a better job of providing three square meals a day and cable TV to fidget felons than each of us could on our own.

And therein lies the key—voluntary submission. We chose to set up a government to serve our collective selves. We chose to do that by giving up our natural right to punish people who steal fidget spinners. Remember, if that forfeiture is not voluntary, then it must be forcible, and that would be a violation of our right to liberty.

Here's where things can get interesting. If we consent to be governed, doesn't it follow that we have the right to un-consent? Well, yes. In fact, we exercise our right to consent and un-consent every election cycle. If we like the people stepping forward to represent us and protect our rights, we vote for them. If they stink, we vote against them and put someone else in charge.

In theory, a government could become so dysfunctional and oppressive that we would have to un-consent in some more overt way. Perhaps the government became so inherently evil that they rigged the election system so that we could not vote out the creeps. That's what the American Revolution was all about. The takeaway is that the government has no authority other than our continuing consent to be governed.

While James Madison is often called "the Father of the Constitution," Madison himself bestowed the title of "penman of the Constitution" on Gouverneur Morris. He represented the state of Pennsylvania at the Constitutional Convention. Credited with writing much of the wording of the Constitution, he was primarily responsible for the famous preamble.

"form a more perfect Union, establish Justice, insure domestic Tranquility, provide for the common defence, promote the general Welfare, and secure the Blessings of Liberty to ourselves and our Posterity."

No, Gouverneur is not one of those old spelling things we mentioned earlier. It's his given first name. Apparently, his mom knew he was destined for greatness.

Republicanism and Democratic Stuff

The neat thing about the Constitution is that it's neither left nor right regarding the current political structure. It just is. There are elements within it that the lefties love and others that the righties revere. And vice versa. Most of the current contentious debate lies in the discussion over how we think things ought to be. This book isn't about how things should be. It's about the Constitution and what it actually says. As you'll see, the Constitution provides the citizenry with ways to specify how they want things to be and make constitutional changes accordingly.

With that said, unless otherwise stated, the use of words including the roots "republican" and "democrat" have nothing to do with the political parties we know today. I think we can all agree that both political organizations have given perfectly good words a bad rap. We'll use them here in the purest sense, as concepts of politics and government. If at some point in this book we need to refer to members of political parties, we'll refer to them as "Democrats" or "Republicans."

The word "republican," used in the context of this book, describes an ideology in which the people hold the power. As opposed to a ruler or ruling class being decided by the lucky sperm club, power and authority are claimed by the citizenry. The concept of republicanism was a big deal during the founding as the whole process was about rejecting monarchy rule and establishing a form of government where the people governed themselves. So if you see a phrase like "Republican Government" in this book, it has nothing to do with political parties, party infighting, or campaign buttons with elephants on them. It has everything to do with the idea of self-government.

While republicanism describes the end result, it doesn't address the "how" part. The other term, democratic, is one term that begins to describe a core principle on which the republican government is designed. The term democratic, as used here, describes the method by which the people make policy decisions. Simply put, "democratic" refers to a system where people vote or otherwise decide on policy and initiatives. There are many variations of democratic systems. A pure democracy is where everybody votes on everything.

Imagine if all of your neighbors had to gather and vote on whether the new folks on the block can plant petunias next to their driveway. That's an example of a pure but dysfunctional democracy. Systems closer to pure democracy were tried by the Athenians back in the day, but the idea fizzled out, in part because trying to make too many decisions by mob or majority rule causes migraines. Besides, how can anyone make a responsible decision while wearing a toga?

The system designed by the founders is a democratic republic or representative democracy. Technically speaking, our system is a constitutional republic, but here we're defining underlying concepts of republicanism and democratic operation. The people use their "republican" power to "democratically" elect representatives who make policy decisions and run the day-to-day business of the society.

And that leads us to the rule book for our constitutional democratic republic.

If you ever find yourself discouraged over the seemingly never-ending bad behavior, loose morals, and lack of ethics exhibited by elected representatives, refer back to Federalist Paper 57. In this one, Publius (James Madison in this case) argues against the accusations that the new government will be run by those who make up the higher echelons of society and may have low regard for the little people.

"The aim of every political constitution is, or ought to be, first to obtain for rulers men who possess most wisdom to discern, and most virtue to pursue, the common good of the society; and in the next place, to take the most effectual precautions for keeping them virtuous whilst they continue to hold their public trust."

There you have it; we're supposed to choose leaders with the most virtue to pursue the common good! Oops.

4

CONSTITUTIONAL WHATS
AND WHYS

"Our constitution protects
aliens, drunks, and U.S.
senators."

— Will Rogers

Ground Rules for Consent-based Government

It's important to note that the Constitution grants nothing to people. It doesn't, and can't, grant rights because we, the people already own those free and clear. As the Declaration of Independence so eloquently states...

> "We hold these truths to be self-evident, that all men are created
> equal, that they are endowed by their Creator with certain
> unalienable Rights, that among these are Life, Liberty and the
> pursuit of Happiness."

The first sentence in the second paragraph of the Declaration of Independence sums up the whole philosophy of the Constitution. If all men are created equal, none can intrude on the rights and liberty of another. None can govern another unless it's by force or via a voluntary arrangement. And since the founders had just vigorously withdrawn from a tsunami of "forcing" by the British, that leaves voluntary consent.

So, the whole reason for the Constitution is to document the ground rules for a consent-based system of government. Since the colonists had just fired the previous government, they had the unique opportunity to design their own, and that turned out to be quite an undertaking.

It's also important to note that the Constitution is just one part of the mix. There are three documents that, together, complete this grand idea of self-government by consent.

When the arguing was done and copies of the Constitution were being prepared for signing, the boys took George Washington out to celebrate at the nearby City Tavern. Apparently, it was quite a party, and we know this because someone saved a copy of the actual bar tab—seriously!

Just some items on the bill for "55 Gentlemans" include the following:

54 Bottles of Madera

60 of Claret ditto

8 ditto of Old Stock

22 Bottles of Porter ditto

8 of Cyder ditto

12 ditto Beer

7 Large Bowels of Punch

The bill also includes line items for broken glasses and decanters. Oh, and that list doesn't include the booze for the musicians—that was itemized separately. Sounds like quite a celebration!

Three Important Parchments

The big three founding documents are the Declaration of Independence, the Constitution, and the Bill of Rights. Let's explore how they complement each other.

It's easiest to think of the Declaration of Independence as the big idea or the thoughts that describe how things ought to be. We'll get into more detail in a later chapter, but for now, think of this document as the gripe about what was wrong with the current system of government under King George. The Declaration describes at a high level the concepts of freedom and goes on to provide an itemized list to the King about everything that's wrong with the current form of colonial rule. While it concludes that revolution is the fix for these problems, it doesn't address the "how-to's" of whatever system will take place after the shooting stops.

The Constitution is the framework of the new government system. It lays out the structure of the new country but doesn't address all the details like whether you can park for free after six pm or on weekends. It doesn't need to because the Constitution defines the system that will make such important decisions. The goal was to design a self-correcting framework that continued to guide the country as it grew. A successful model would guarantee liberty to citizens, well, forever.

You might think of the Bill of Rights as a check and balance against the interpretation of the Constitution. While the Constitution is designed to be simple and crystal clear, there was more than a little concern that future generations of reality TV watchers might lose track of essential principles and allow the government to become lazy about their responsibility to protect natural rights.

As an extra layer of protection, the Bill of Rights presents a list of negative liberties or things the government cannot do. For example, even though the whole point of the shooting war and subsequent Constitutional Convention was to protect liberty, the folks who wrote this stuff down added insurance. Consider as an example the First Amendment. The First Amendment doesn't grant a "right" to free speech and religious worship; it prohibits Congress from making laws that violate freedom of expression and freedom of religion.

These three documents together provide the complete package—the why, the how, and the checks and balances.

There are precisely two members in one of history's most exclusive clubs. Can you name the dynamic duo that signed each of the Declaration of Independence, the Articles of Confederation, and the Constitution? Give up? Those two individuals are Robert Morris, who coordinated the financing of the American Revolution and Roger Sherman from Connecticut.

What is the Constitution?

A constitution is a contract. It's also a rule book. One could also describe it as an etiquette guide in which bad manners are answered with real consequences. In short, it outlines the expected behaviors of all parties involved in the consent-based government discussed in the previous chapter.

The easy way to think about a constitution of a consent-based government system is to compare it to a lawn mowing service contract with little Jimmy Husqvarna down the street. Yes, I chose an analogy where a 12-year-old plays the role of our government on purpose. It's in everyone's best interest for your lawn to get cut regularly. It's in your best interest to focus on important things like arranging the food in your pantry alphabetically rather than laboring behind a lawnmower. It's in your neighborhood association's best interest for your lawn to be maintained so they don't have to send nasty letters. And last but not least, it's in your 12-year-old neighbor's best interest to make 25 bucks so he can buy the latest edition of Grand Theft Auto.

So, if we want to model modern little league soccer and make everyone a winner, we must establish a contract. While it may not be written down, it's still an agreement. The kid agrees to mow the lawn. You agree to pay him. The neighborhood home owner's association becomes depressed because they have no reason to send you nasty letters. Almost everyone is happy because all parties voluntarily consent to this mutually beneficial arrangement.

But what happens if your adolescent horticulturist fails? Maybe he's stuck on level 19 of Assassin's Creed and can't get away from the X-Box, or perhaps he finally left the basement and discovered girls. Whatever the cause, since you have a consent-based contract, it's your prerogative to find another teenage lawn hand. You voluntarily agreed to hire that little weasel who only edges every other week, so you can voluntarily agree to un-hire him too.

The Constitution is a voluntary consent contract between the people and the government. The people agree to be governed because it makes sense. Still, the government has to behave because the people are only voluntarily agreeing to be governed as long as the government doesn't act like a weenie. That sounds like circular logic, and in a sense, it is. That's OK, however, because the circle can be broken for cause.

James Madison was a busy guy during the Constitutional Convention. Not only did he do the summer reading and come prepared with an outline, but he also took copious notes during the entire proceedings. After his death, the government purchased his journal for the sum of $30,000. That was a lot of coin back in 1837. The level of detail of who said what when makes for fascinating reading.

As to the rule book concept, the Constitution sets forth exactly how the government will operate. Not only does it define the structure of the government, but it also clarifies the limits of power granted by the people to the government. Getting back to little Jimmy Husqvarna, it's analogous to our lawn mowing agreement specifying that he'll edge and trim every week, use only a Fisher-Price-approved lawnmower and promise not to dump the grass clippings on the neighbors' lawns.

The Constitution is primarily written in such a way that all authority is assumed to belong to the people except that which is expressly granted to the government by the language in the Constitution. Technically, if the Constitution doesn't establish government authority, then it doesn't exist. That's in theory, of course, because we all know how much the government's role and authority have bloated over the past 200 years.

Why We Have a Constitition

Why do we have a Constitution? That's simple. By law, politicians must have principles they can wantonly violate and ignore. The Constitution makes a convenient place from which they can draw material.

But seriously, the key word in our somewhat frivolous explanation is "principles." The Constitution is all about timeless principles, not timely policies. This is the root of much debate over whether the Constitution is still relevant after all these years. If it were a document of policies, it wouldn't be. However, it's a document of principles, and that's a critical distinction. What's the difference between a principle and a policy? Let's ask Merriam-Webster.

Principle (prin·ci·ple)
> *noun*
> - a comprehensive and fundamental law, doctrine, or assumption
> - a rule or code of conduct

Policy (pol·i·cy)
> *noun*
> - management or procedure based primarily on material interest
> - a definite course or method of action selected from among alternatives and in light of given conditions to guide and determine present and future decisions
> - a high-level overall plan embracing the general goals and acceptable procedures, especially of a governmental body

What's all that mean? Principles like the natural right to free speech and freedom of religion don't change, but specific policies do. That's why the Constitution so carefully lays out the infrastructure and process for making policy decisions and laws.

Knowing that the only thing constant is change, the founders recognized the futility of drafting a set of specific rules and regulations. Imagine if we had a pile of regulations and instructions in the Constitution about churning butter, flying kites in lightning storms, and illegal uses for wig powder. Instead of trying to detail the specific rules in advance, they focused on implementing a system designed to protect timeless principles by creating a system of decision making. Decisions could be made under the constitutional framework and changed based on current and future environments.

As we'll see when we get into the text of the Constitution itself, much thought went into the system that should make, change, and even repeal specific laws over the decades and centuries. While frustrating on occasion—OK, maybe daily—that system is specifically designed to encourage careful deliberation and compromise. It's also designed to discourage rash reactions or mob rule policies that may flare up from time to time.

So, what underlying principles is the Constitution designed to protect over the long haul? We've talked at length about life, liberty, and the pursuit of happiness, so those are easy ones. There are also structural principles, such as the respective roles of federal and state governments.

For example, as you read through the Constitution itself, you might note its emphasis on what the federal government's role should be. If you sense a cautionary tone when reading about the feds, that's because of the underlying assumption that states must maintain most of the power.

The federal government was never intended to become the primary authority over our daily lives. It was only supposed to handle issues that states could not efficiently address independently, like foreign policy. Imagine the red-tape nightmare if every state had to make its own trade agreements with France. The price of croissants would go through the roof, and Louisiana would probably corner the market on Beaujolais Nouveau.

Of course, foreign policy goes beyond trade agreements. Without the security of the union as a whole, the states can't do a very good job of protecting liberty and personal rights. Wrap your head around this "what-if" scenario. If Lichtenstein invaded Vermont and no other states came to their defense because they'd figured out how to make their own breakfast syrup, what might stop France from invading Monkey's Eyebrow, Kentucky? And yes, that's a real place, not to mention a national treasure.

There's a lot going on behind the scenes in the Constitution beyond the high-level roles of federal and state governments. It also meticulously lays out the design and operating principles of how the government should function.

As the functional mechanisms of government often seem nuts when you watch how it operates, you might ask why the system was created the way it was. Why does the Constitution establish three distinct branches of government? Why does it create an arguably dysfunctional legislative body to make all the rules? Why is legislative conflict "built-in" to our system?

The answer is simple in its elegance. The Constitution documents a system that allows majority rule without the traditional pitfalls of majority rule.

While that sounds like a typo at first read, it's not. When a 51% majority makes all decisions, things tend to spin out of control pretty quickly. Those in the 49% block have no representation whatsoever. The result is a type of majority tyranny—another situation the founders wanted to avoid.

One of the big reasons that the Constitution so carefully outlines a representative form of democracy is to protect the rights of the minority while following the general principles set by the majority.

Since the Constitution plants principles in place like big stakes in the ground, neither a simple majority nor the minority can undo those. As we'll see later, there are ways to change the Constitution itself, but that process requires a significant super-majority, so a lot of us have to be in agreement before a sweeping principle change becomes binding.

You can get away with pretty much anything and still run for office. The seventh President of the United States, Andrew Jackson, reportedly fought in over 100 duels, most of which were over insults to his wife. Well, at least it was for a good cause! He was shot twice over the years, but hey, 98-2 is a pretty good record.

Is the Constitution Binding?

What happens if the government misbehaves? The second paragraph of the Declaration of Independence speaks directly to that point.

> *"That whenever any form of Government becomes destructive of these ends, it is the right of the people to alter or to abolish it, and to institute new Government...."*

That's the primary reason the colonists flipped a collective bird to King George. They felt that a just government should be accountable to its initial consent arrangement. When the colonists filed complaints that their current government was no longer serving them justly, George said fuhgeddaboudit. So, the colonists replaced him with a new government of their choosing.

Clearly, running around replacing governments all the time is not something you want to take as lightly as finding new lawn-mowing teens. The Declaration of Independence also speaks clearly to that point, reserving the whole rebellion thing for seriously onerous situations. That's part of the reason our system so carefully defines the process of frequent local elections. The idea is that if our representatives are stinking up Washington, then we can easily tell them to buzz off without going through all the trouble of another civil war. To a large extent, it's a peaceful and self-correcting system — by design.

If you're tired of government shenanigans, you can always do what a group of citizens from Pennsylvania did and propose a constitutional amendment to do away with both the Senate and the Presidency. Apparently, those voters were tired of how politicians "always advanced the interest of the money, railroad, and manufacturing speculators to the prejudice of the common welfare." Needless to say, this proposed amendment didn't get far.

5

THE DECLARATION OF INDEPENDENCE

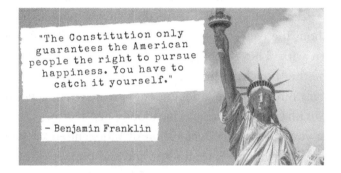

"The Constitution only guarantees the American people the right to pursue happiness. You have to catch it yourself."

– Benjamin Franklin

Theory of the Declaration

The Declaration of Independence is the document that answers the question of why a new government was needed. The Constitution outlines the structure of that government and how it works. Put a different way, the purpose of the Declaration of Independence is to provide a statement of the way things ought to be, and the Constitution is like an owner's manual for a brand new government.

Thomas Jefferson sums up the purpose of the Declaration of Independence perfectly in a letter to one of his fans, Henry Lee, on May 8, 1825.

"When forced, therefore, to resort to arms for redress, an appeal to the tribunal of the world was deemed proper for our justification. This was the object of the Declaration of Independence. Not to find out new principles, or new arguments, never before thought of, not merely to say things which had never been said before; but to place before mankind the common sense of the subject, in terms so plain and firm as to command their assent, and to justify ourselves in the independent stand we are compelled to take."

The Declaration of Independence was, in one way, a justification to other nations. As liberty and freedom were universally understood to be human rights, the world at large would understand why the Americans rebelled against the Brits.

And what were those obvious reasons? For eons, or at least as far back as Cicero (106 - 43 B.C.), freedom-loving people have been talking about the concept of natural human rights. These are rights we're born with. They're not granted by any person or government. They're neither bought online nor are they a prize for reaching level 297 of Angry Birds. They're independent of the current governmental structure in place at the time and location of one's birth.

When you look at the Declaration of Independence, three "natural rights" are evident—life, liberty, and the pursuit of happiness. Two other natural rights appear in the Virginia Declaration of Rights dated June 12, 1776. First, all people have the right to acquire and possess property. Second, people have the right to free expression of religion.

So these five natural rights, life, liberty, the pursuit of happiness, the right to acquire and possess property, and the freedom to exercise religion, are built-in. There is no requirement to send in the warranty card or register to activate our rights. You and I have them, no matter what.

Since these rights are natural and pre-existing, no one can take them away, except, of course, by force. As we all know, that's happened plenty because we never seem to be lacking a proper bully. There's one other way we can give up or lose our rights. Remember what that is? That's by voluntary consent. Since they're my rights, I can do what I want with them. I can't mess with anyone else's natural rights, but I can give up my own if I choose.

This is where the Colonists' view of proper government comes into play. It's considered beneficial for people to band together and create communities. When people band together for the purpose of benefitting all, then some form of government becomes a necessity. A "government" can provide security and protection of everyone's natural rights. But for it to work, there has to be some basic authority structure. And for someone or something to have authority over another, the "another" has to voluntarily submit or be forced.

So, under a proper model of government, we all volunteer to "give up" some of our natural rights and agree to be governed. Since it's a voluntary arrangement, we can "un-volunteer" at any time if the government becomes oppressive or fails to perform its duties.

At a very high level, that's the theory underlying the parting of ways from the British as written in the Declaration of Independence. We volunteered our natural rights to the Crown for everyone's bene-fit. They became oppressive and abused our natural rights. We chose to dump them and form a new and improved government.

Gad Hitchcock, a notable pastor in the Pembroke area outside of Boston, delivered a whopper of a political sermon for Election Day, 1774. As it turned out, British General Thomas Gage, the British military governor of the Province of Massachusetts Bay, was in the house that day to hear Gad's message about the virtues of consent-based government. By the way, consent-based government was the polar opposite of what was happening in the colonies at the time. Can you say awkward?

"In such a government, rulers have their distinct powers assigned them by the people, who are the only source of civil authority on earth, with the view of having them exercised for the public advantage; and in proportion as this worthy end of their investiture is kept in sight, and pros-ecuted, the bands of society are strengthened, and its interests promoted..."

Since it was considered bad form for British Officers to shoot at pastors during their sermons, Hitchcock survived the service to preach another day.

What the Declaration of Independence Says

Earlier, we discussed how the Declaration of the Causes and Necessity of Taking Up Arms was somewhat like a nasty letter to your cable provider. The Declaration has some elements of that too, but at the end, instead of threatening to switch to satellite, the Colonists informed the King that they were "outta here" altogether.

Scholars outline the Declaration of Independence differently, but I will explain it by breaking it into six main topical areas. Later in the book, we've included the full text of the Declaration of Independence so you can check it out in its original form.

Like something out of a Mission Impossible *movie, the Constitution, Bill of Rights, and Declaration of Independence are stored in a 50-ton fireproof, waterproof, and at least partially nuclear-bomb-proof vault under their exhibit hall in the National Archives building. Each morning before the hall opens to the public, the sealed display cases are raised into their viewing portals. Each night, they are lowered back into the protective vault. The actual storage cases are helium-filled and kept at a temperature of 70 degrees with a humidity of 25 to 30 percent. In case of emergency or threat, security personnel can lower the document cases back into the underground cave.*

1. Sit down and listen. Things are about to get real.

*"When in the Course of human events it becomes necessary for one
    people to dissolve the political bands which have connected
    them with another...
...they should declare the causes which impel them to the
    separation."*

The preamble to the Declaration of Independence explains that, as gentlemen, it's polite and respectful to offer reasons for severance from your friends and family. The preamble is somewhat akin to a high school public speaking class. You know, to start a proper speech, you tell them what you're going to tell them right up front.

2. George... This is really obvious stuff, why don't you get it?

> *"We hold these truths to be self-evident, that all men are created equal, that they are endowed by their Creator with certain unalienable Rights, that among these are Life, Liberty and the pursuit of Happiness."*

The document outlines man's natural and inalienable rights and suggests that the purpose of government is to secure these rights but only under the consent of those governed. Since people voluntarily consent to be governed, it is their right, and actually, their duty, to separate from any government that does not honor and secure their natural rights.

Translation: "George, we've had enough of your crap. We're leaving your stinky government and making a better one of our own."

3. An epic rant...

> *"To prove this, let Facts be submitted to a candid world.*
> *He has refused his Assent to Laws, the most wholesome and neces-sary for the public good.*
> *He has forbidden his Governors to pass Laws of immediate and pressing importance unless suspended in their operation till his Assent should be obtained; and when so suspended, he has utterly neglected to attend to them."*

And so on...

And the long list of grievances against the King begins. Twenty-seven of them, in fact. If Facebook had been invented, this would have been a truly epic online political rant worthy of much un-friending. Interestingly, the grievances were made directly against the King and not Parliament, even though the Houses had the real political power at the time. Part of the reason for addressing King George personally was to poke a finger in the eye of the whole "monarchy by birth" thing.

4. Our patience is running thin!

> *"In every stage of these Oppressions We have Petitioned for Redress in the most humble terms: Our repeated Petitions have been answered only by repeated injury."*

We've asked nicely. We've begged, pleaded, and even offered to wash your carriage and goat sit, yet you continue to dis us.

5. We're outta here!

> *"We, therefore, the Representatives of the United States of America, in General Congress, Assembled, appealing to the Supreme Judge of the world for the rectitude of our intentions, do, in the Name, and by Authority of the good People of these Colonies, solemnly publish and declare, That these united Colonies are, and of Right ought to be Free and Independent States, that they are Absolved from all Allegiance to the British Crown, and that all political connection between them and the State of Great Britain, is and ought to be totally dissolved..."*

Here's the money section if you've been wondering where the country got its name. As you might guess, it's where the signers declared themselves an independent country free from rule by the British Crown.

6. Grand Opening!

> *"...have full Power to levy War, conclude Peace, contract Alliances,*

establish Commerce, and to do all other Acts and Things which
Independent States may of right do."

The final clause in the Declaration of Independence is a statement to the rest of the world that the new United States of America is open. Subject to regular business hours, the country is now available to make treaties, trade agreements, and wage war if so inclined.

If you're paying close attention, you might do a double-take on the "all men are created equal" phrase. Why? Because at the time that was writ-ten, slavery still existed, both throughout the British Empire as a whole and in the American Colonies. Most of the Founding Fathers, even slave owners like Washington and Jefferson, were committed to ending the prac-tice. That's a long story, so we'll get into more detail about that later.

6

HOW THE CONSTITUTION CAME TO BE

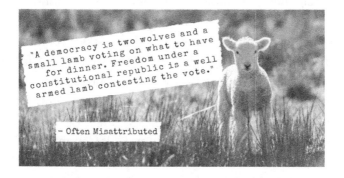

"A democracy is two wolves and a small lamb voting on what to have for dinner. Freedom under a constitutional republic is a well armed lamb contesting the vote."

— Often Misattributed

Labor Pains: Birthing a Constitution

In a stunning revelation that the federal government has never been considered a model of competence and efficiency, Alexander Hamilton began his Federalist Number 1 letter, *"After an unequivocal experience of the inefficacy of the subsisting federal government, you are called upon to deliberate on a new Constitution for the United States of America."* In other words, the system we tried before sucked eggs, so we need to figure out a better plan.

The Constitution was signed on September 17, 1787. It was signed in the Pennsylvania State House, the same place where the Declaration of Inde-

pendence was inked. It also happens to be where George Washington
received his commission as Commander of the Continental Army.

Baby Steps: The Articles of Confederation

While not originally intended as such, the Articles of Confederation became a "pre-Constitution." Why didn't it make the final cut? It was a failure. On the bright side, it brought to light design flaws that would later be corrected in the actual Constitution.

Try to imagine a cooperative scenario more dysfunctional than a neighborhood homeowners' association. Let me help. What if you lived in a community, say Enchanted Estates, where each homeowner does whatever the heck they want on their own property? Sounds great, doesn't it? It is right up to the point where everyone wants to build a neighborhood badminton court. The fundraising process alone would be like a group of partygoers throwing money on the table to pay the bar tab. You know how that works. Everyone tosses in "more than their share," yet the total always comes up far short. I think we can all agree that if one or two out of every ten homes voluntarily kicked in some coin to pay for the badminton courts, that would be a shockingly good result.

Now imagine if the Glamorous Palms Golf Community, down the road, waged war to take over the Enchanted Estates community pool. Who in your neighborhood would organize the defense? More importantly, who would listen to anyone who stepped up to the task? Since it's unlikely most residents would have tanks and Humvees in their garages, how would our neighborhood pay for the big guns needed to fend off hordes of marauding golf carts?

This scenario isn't all that far off the mark of the original Articles of Confederation. Simply put, it was a loose and primarily voluntary agreement between the states. On November 15, 1777, Congress passed the Articles of Confederation and sent the document to the 13 states for ratification. The process took a whopping three and a half years for all the states to agree to this weak and ineffective agreement. It was finally adopted on March 1, 1781.

Why all the difficulty? The people involved had just moved away from the neighborhood association from hell, so the idea of voluntarily creating a new one with any power whatsoever was not at all appealing. Since the states were very skittish about giving up any of their power to a central authority, the result was a highly dysfunctional figurehead national government. Kind of like now.

Knowing the problems inherent in the Articles of Confederation is a fundamental background to understanding why the Constitution is what it is, so let's take a brief look at some challenges.

There's a road paved with good intentions, and it might lead right to Article III. This section opens with the following:

> *"The said states hereby severally enter into a firm league of friendship with each other...."*

See the problem? While the Constitution also relies on voluntary submission to government, the Articles of Confederation didn't have quite enough submission, instead relying on friendship and good intentions more than an adequate dose of enumerated powers to get the job done.

The Articles of Confederation offered no provision for an executive leader (like a president), government agencies to deal with the daily business of running the country, or a national judicial branch to resolve disputes that crossed state lines. Oh, and there was no authority to raise taxes, and while at first glance that could be seen as a big win, there were plenty of Revolutionary War debts to pay. States weren't all that keen on paying those bills under a voluntary system, so interest piled up. Remember the bar tab scenario?

However, it wasn't just a national debt issue that brought the inadequacies of the Articles of Confederation to the forefront. To grossly oversimplify the post-Revolutionary War economic situation:

- New European trading partners wanted to deal in hard currency when doing business with the new nation, probably because the country had no credit reputation.
- There was little real hard currency to go around.

- Veterans of the war were habitually underpaid or not paid at all and accumulated piles of personal debt.
- Creditors also wanted hard currency, but no one had it to pay them either.
- States and the Continental Congress printed all sorts of paper currency, which quickly became massively devalued and worth only the paper on which it was printed.
- Chaos ensues. People can't pay debts, taxes, or cable bills. Lots of hard-working folks get repo visits on their livestock, homes, and farms, and many are tossed in jail. There was general unhappiness in the land.
- Add in some political corruption and cronyism (some things never change), and conditions were ripe to figure out a better way.

All of this financial chaos led to violence. Revolutionary War veteran Daniel Shays got so upset that he recruited over 4,000 other hacked-off farmers to take over the Armory in Springfield, Massachusetts, with the aim of overthrowing the government. Having reached a boiling point, conditions were ripe to convene a new Constitutional Convention.

There was one big benefit to the Articles of Confederation. It gave the new country its name.

Article I. The Stile of this confederacy shall be, "The United States of America."

The Constitutional Convention

Modern presidents get all braggy about getting some big piece of legislation passed during their first 100 days in office. Back in 1787, people must have been far more productive. In just over 100 days, the delegates to the Constitutional Convention designed a whole country and even wrote down all the rules—by hand.

Fifty-five delegates from 12 states gathered at the Pennsylvania State House near the end of May 1787 to hammer out an agreement for an improved working relationship between the newly independent collection of states.

Rhode Island didn't send any delegates because it had a hissy fit and believed the convention was an attempt to overthrow the existing form of government. It was, more or less, but that wasn't necessarily a bad thing as the current plan wasn't working out all that well. They weren't the only ones who were skeptical of the process. In fact, Patrick Henry, the famous patriot who gave that "Give me liberty, or give me death!" speech after drinking lots of beer with Samuel Adams, chose not to participate in the convention. Why? He "smelt a rat." More specifically, he was concerned about the process being some kind of power play by those who wanted a powerful national government.

As the proceedings started, Revolutionary War Chief Financial Officer Robert Morris resorted to a proven winner and nominated George Washington to serve as President of the Constitutional Convention. Having refined his skills at tobacco growing, nighttime river crossings, and looking manly on dollar bills, Washington seemed an excellent choice to unite the skeptical and opinionated bunch. After a unanimous vote in favor of Washington, the group immediately adjourned for lunch, as politicians tend to do.

As you might expect when gathering a bunch of hot-headed Patriots to hash out a deal, things were contentious for a while. Remember, these guys didn't just argue politics; they had just finished a shooting war over political issues. Regarding commitment, today's social media justice warriors have nothing on the guys who wore tights and wigs. Many delegates came with preconceived ideas about how the Constitution should be shaped.

For example, James Madison, representing the great state of Virginia, arrived early prepared with a slew of ideas that he and the other delegates from the Old Dominion state had worked out. Known as the Virginia Plan, many of its ideas survived the debate and made it to the final draft. For example, the Virginia plan included the concept of dual legislative houses, each with a different "loyalty," so to speak. As the legislature would have massive power to create laws, the idea was to make the process as deliberative as possible.

The Virginia Plan also included provisions for a national judicial branch and the concept of veto power. That Madison came prepared with all these ideas was arguably one reason that so much progress was made during the 100-day slugfest. Not only did it kick off the debate along specific topical lines and bypass the normal "where are we going to start" and group shrugging phases, the Virginia delegation scored a significant victory in getting their ideas adopted. Having arrived prepared, the debate was launched on terms of the Virginians' choosing.

Nothing is ever easy, and the first big potential convention derailment popped up with the Virginia Plan's concept of proportional representation by states based on their population. Large states would have more Congress Critters and, therefore, would make most of the rules. Smaller states weren't too keen on the idea since the previous Articles of Confederation had been operating (although dysfunctionally) under a "one vote per state" system.

After much pushing, shoving, name-calling, and threats to take their balls and go home, Roger Sherman from Connecticut presented a compromise. The body, now known as the House of Representatives, would be composed of delegates from each state where said number was based on population. However, in the Senate, each state would have equal representation. In James Madison's comprehensive notes during the convention, he wrote on June 11, 1787, that Sherman said, "The smaller States would never agree to the plan on any other principle than an equality of suffrage in this branch." It took a few more weeks of haggling, but this agreement, known as the Connecticut Compromise, kept the process moving forward. Until...

On June 18, 1787, New York delegate Alexander Hamilton gave a speech proposing some surprising ideas. Among them were creating an office of president—for life—and giving that person absolute veto power. Hamilton called the British government, which the delegates had just left, "the best in the world." Some of his proposals sounded an awful lot like a monarchy. Interestingly, later on, during the ratification stage, Hamilton became one of the greatest proponents of the new Constitution.

The next debate over population-based representation surfaced concerning slavery. Slave states wanted slaves to count, at least to determine representation in Congress. Many free states wanted to end slavery altogether, so they had no interest in allowing the number of slaves in a state to influence the number of congressional representatives from slave states. They also had concerns about increased importation of slaves changing the balance of power in Congress due to the effect that would have on population numbers.

Add to that mix the issue of counting population for taxation, and opposing desires come into play. Plenty of other matters, including fears of export tariffs that could destroy southern economies, confused discussions until, at last, a significant compromise was achieved. Slaves would count as three-fifths of a person for representation and taxation, so slave states would gain seats in Congress while also paying taxes for slaves. Another part of the deal called for the practice of importing new slaves to end by 1808. Was everyone happy? No. In reality, few were happy, but a deal had been reached to overcome one of the convention's biggest obstacles.

On September 17, 1787, two days after a successful vote, the Constitution was signed by 39 of the original 55 delegates. Some delegates left during the process, and a couple refused to sign as a statement of protest, but it was a done deal — at least until copies were delivered to the states for ratification.

The Ratification Process Begins

One hundred and thirteen days (more or less, depending on how you count) of bickering in the sweltering summer confines of Independence Hall was nothing compared to the ratification fight to come. Besides the typical and expected discussions during happy hour, proponents of both sides (ratification or not) resorted to writing each other letters in the newspapers. Many papers across the country picked up on the debate and published these letters.

As we'll see in Article VII of the Constitution itself, nine states had to ratify its contents for it to become binding across the land. If you're paying close attention to the numbers, that works out to just over 69 percent of the 13 states in existence at the time.

The ratification process officially began on September 28, 1787, when Congress delivered copies of the proposed Constitution to all 13 states. It didn't take long for things to move. By early January 1788, five states (Delaware, Pennsylvania, New Jersey, Georgia, and Connecticut) had already approved the measure. But then things got sticky.

Delegates, voters, and state Constitutional Convention partygoers had pledged allegiance to two rival gangs: the Federalists and the Anti-Federalists. The Federalists were supportive of a more powerful central government. However, in their wildest nightmares, few of them would be pleased with the extent of power our modern government has assumed. The Anti-Federalists were concerned about preserving individual and states' rights against the onslaught of a powerful Fedzilla.

The net result of the disagreements between these rivals was that the Federalists believed the Constitution was good to go "as is." The Anti-Federalists generally wanted to see a Bill of Rights included in the Constitution before they would fully support ratification. Hold that thought; we'll get into more details shortly.

In a continuing effort to be ornery, Rhode Island rejected the terms of the Constitution on March 24, 1788. In the end, it didn't mean much, as more than enough states agreed to the terms. As a side note, Rhode Island finally got on board with the program in late May 1790. Oh, "Rogue Island" didn't exactly do this voluntarily, but only after a new Senate resolution passed proposing to ban all trade with the uncooperative state.

The War of the Letters

"We want small government!"
The Federalists
"No! We want an even smaller government!"
The Anti-Federalists

If you think arguing about politics started with the invention of Facebook, forget it. The founders were the masters of the written put down even though they didn't have the benefit of social media memes. At the time, all political debate had to be done in the form of letters to the editors of newspapers. And I do mean letters; handwritten ones laboriously scribed with a sharpened goose feather. Anyway, these "letters to the editor" were one of the primary methods of making the case to the public for the adoption (or not) of the new Constitution. This collection of letters became known as the Federalist Papers.

So, what were the Federalist Papers? To sway the citizens of New York and other states to ratify the new Constitution, a writer identified as "Publius" wrote a series of 85 essays published in three different New York newspapers between 1787 and 1788. The Federalist Papers represent the "pro-Constitution" side of a considerable debate between guys who wanted small government and other guys who wanted even smaller government. Oh, by the way, "Publius" was a pen name for three different wise men: Alexander Hamilton, James Madison, and John Jay.

On the flip side were the Anti-Federalist letters. While not having a catchy name like "The Federalist Papers," this movement expressed the opposite view that the Constitution should not be ratified, at least not in its current form. Anti-Federalist essays were authored by aspiring politicians identified as Brutus, Centinel, and Federal Farmer, to name a few. In fact, Patrick Henry was a vocal Anti-Federalist. That's not surprising when you remember he chose not to attend the Constitutional Convention because he "smelt a rat."

The whole debate was an issue of degree. Many believed that too little government was a danger to liberty because a lack of rules and order would prevent the protection of individual rights. If the government were too big and powerful, like the one they had just kicked out, then individual liberties could be abused by power-hungry bullies.

The trick would be finding the right balance where the government is powerful enough to provide national security, enforce laws related to commerce and contracts, and provide a system for dealing with those who interfere with the natural rights of their fellow citizens. However, the government had to be small and "weak" enough to defend against man's natural tendency to exert power over others when in positions of influence. After all, all governments are, by definition, staffed with imperfect humans. If the government had too much power, then bad behavior could lead to tyranny.

To set the stage for the Federalist vs. Anti-Federalist debate, one must remember that all involved had just fought a major war to obtain liberty and freedom from an oppressive government. With so many people thinking along these lines, most didn't see a need for the Constitution to contain a separate itemization of individual rights. The concepts of individual liberty and government subservience to its citizens were thought to be so indisputable that they didn't need to be written down.

However, the anti-federalists expressed concern that, down the road, a growing government might become too big for their britches, so it would be essential to document a set of limitations on governmental power against the individual. If you don't write down the rules, they tend to change over time. The abuses of British authority were fresh on the minds of the Anti-Federalists, and they wanted an insurance policy against similar behavior in the future.

Before we get into the Federalist and Anti-Federalists arguments, we should note some early disagreement over each group's respective labels. Both sides thought of themselves as "federalists" in the pure sense of the word and tried to claim the "federalist" title as their own. The group we now know as the Federalists won the shouting match, so for clarity, we'll use the traditional historical labels here—Federalists and Anti-Federalists.

Who signed the Constitution? Well, a total of 39 people did, but some big names didn't for various reasons. Thomas Jefferson was Minister to France at the time, and since fax hadn't yet been invented, his name is not on it. John Adams was serving in Great Britain. That must have been a bit awkward. Three others refused to sign it: Elbridge Gerry, Edmund Randolph, and George Mason. Benjamin Franklin was a signer and had the distinction of being the oldest at age 81.

The Federalist View

In a long series of arguments via these essays, the Federalists presented the case for establishing a Federal government with real power beyond that provided by the Articles of Confederation.

So, what did the Federalist Papers say? The series of essays aimed to expose the flaws inherent in the existing Articles of Confederation, demonstrate how the new Constitution provided the necessary corrections, and rebut concerns over the structure of the proposed government. Actually, correction is too weak a word as the Constitution was really a wholesale replacement for the Articles of Confederation. The Federalist Papers made the case that a robust Federal Government was the only way to secure liberty, provide national security, and position the country for growth and westward expansion.

The Federalists felt that the underlying ideas in the Constitution itself provided plenty of protection. In Federalist 84, Publius (in this case Alexander Hamilton) made arguments to that effect. He writes, *"the Constitution proposed by the convention contains, as well as the Constitution of this state, a number of such provisions."*

In addition to the fact state constitutions included forms of "bills of rights," he called upon specific examples of how the new Constitution itself protects against tyranny. For example, Article I, Section 9 establishes that habeas corpus will not be unduly suspended. Article IV includes other important protection concepts like the right to a trial by jury. Throw the ban against nobility into the mix, and the thinking was, "what could possibly go wrong?"

Speaking of nobility, another reason there was significant opposition to documenting a separate Bill of Rights was the historical uses of such a document. In the past, an instrument like this had been used to "carve out" specific rights of subjects from the implied authority of royalty. Contrary to the intent of the Constitution, a "bill of rights" would, in a sense, flip the Constitution on its ear by implying the government had all rights and power except for those specifically enumerated.

When you boil everything down, the Federalists believed that the entire model of the new United States negated the need for a specific Bill of Rights because the people would hold all the power. If we're all in charge, and we're the ones to place and remove individuals from power, then how could the government misbehave?

Hamilton puts it this way. *"Here, in strictness, the people surrender nothing; and as they retain everything they have no need of particular reservations."* Hamilton also expressed concern that creating a list of rules and restrictions might imply that the government has authority that it doesn't actually have. When you tell a bully that he can't steal your Little Debbie's snack money, you're, in a sense admitting that he can do so in the first place.

Two presidents signed the Constitution: George Washington and James Madison.

The Anti-Federalist View

On the opposite side, the Anti-Federalists foresaw the invention of reality TV and realized that as citizens became less engaged in government affairs in favor of watching *America's Funniest Videos*, they might neither know nor care about the day-to-day behavior of government. Without vigorous and engaged oversight by voluntarily-governed folk, bureaucrats might gradually assume and exert more and more unjust authority. Ring a bell?

The Anti-Federalists expressed two layers of concern: protection of individual liberties and preservation of power at the state level. Having endured being subjects of a monarchy, the Anti-Federalists had legitimate concerns about a powerful central government led by a president, sliding down the slippery slope only to crash into a new monarchy under a different name. Would the president gradually assume the role of a United States King? It was a genuine concern.

There was also plenty of angst over the erosion of state power and the creation of a federal judicial branch. Remember the Intolerable Acting we talked about earlier in the book? The Administration of Justice Act effectively removed adjudication of disputes from the location where the dispute arose and placed judicial power far away.

Anti-Federalists were concerned a federal court system might do the same thing.

The bottom line was that the Anti-Federalists opposed the adoption of the new Constitution, at least in its current form. Sure, some were happy to continue to operate under the existing Articles of Confederation or at least an updated version of it. Others were open to adopting the new Constitution as long as it contained a Bill of Rights that clearly spelled out protections for individuals and state governments. You'll see this quite clearly when we look at the 10th Amendment later in the book.

The Constitutional Convention proceedings of 1787 were secret, and few outside knew the direction that the new Constitution would take. On completion, a local woman, identified as Mrs. Powel, asked Benjamin Franklin, "Well, Doctor, what have we got, a republic or a monarchy?" Franklin's response? "A republic, if you can keep it."

Closing the Deal

While the first five states ratified the new Constitution pretty quickly, the Federalist vs. Anti-Federalist feud stalled the process at the Massachusetts Ratification Convention. Federalists wanted a simple up or down ratification vote on the Constitution as it was written. Anti-Federalists wanted to change the Constitution to include a Bill of Rights.

In a move that became known as the Massachusetts Compromise, two Anti-Federalists, one with excellent penmanship and the other with a fine ale, John Hancock and Samuel Adams, helped craft a compromise. The basic idea was that the Anti-Federalists (at least some of them anyway) would support ratification of the Constitution but with the understanding that the new Congress would pass a Bill of Rights. That deal got enough votes to push passage forward in Massachusetts.

New Hampshire completed the technical portion of the ratification effort, accepting the Constitution on June 21, 1788. Keep in mind that there were still some large states, including Virginia and New

York, that had not yet ratified, so in practicality, the job was not yet complete. Virginia ratified the Constitution on June 25, and New York finished up about a month later on July 26.

When all the dust had settled, the Federalists vs. Anti-Federalists match ended in a tie. The Federalists got the Constitution ratified, which might appear to be a win. It was. But the Anti-Federalists didn't lose. They also got what many on their side wanted—a Bill of Rights. It just happened almost immediately after the ratification of the new Constitution. New President George Washington sent copies of the 12 proposed amendments to the states on October 2, 1789. By December 15, 1791, three-fourths of the states had ratified ten amendments, and the Bill of Rights became official.

While the creation of the Constitution was a group project, James Madison was arguably the "Father of the Constitution." While he held opinions on the Federalist side of the debate, he quickly saw that adding a Bill of Rights was a political necessity. Without the promise of that bonus feature, it is unlikely that the Constitution would have been ratified in its original form. He jumped in with both feet and was instrumental in crafting and pitching the first 12 constitutional amendments, 10 of which were ratified by the states to become the Bill of Rights as we know it today.

7

WHAT DOES THE CONSTITUTION SAY?

"A republic, if you can keep it."

~ Ben Franklin

"Well, Doctor, what have we got, a republic or a monarchy?"

- Mrs. Powel

Constitution by the Numbers

We're going to walk through the Constitution and explore what it says—by the numbers. To keep things less messy than those do-it-yourself painting kits, we'll break it into small chunks by article and section.

It's a good time to point out there are two elements determining how the Constitution applies to our daily lives. First, there's the raw text of the Constitution itself. We're going to cover that here, section by section. The second influence on the practical meaning of the Constitution is case law. Over the past couple of hundred years, thousands of court cases have tested, challenged, clarified, and otherwise weighed in on what various sections of the Constitution mean and how they apply.

The language of the Constitution itself is short and sweet. Paper records from the court cases that test its meaning could fill the Great Lakes. So, remember that what may look supremely simple and obvious might not be once the lawyers have gotten to it. While we'll hit on a couple of significant case law interpretation issues here and there where appropriate, there's not a book thick enough to cover it all. So, we're going to focus on the original text rather than modern case law interpretation.

The main body of the Constitution is comprised of seven parts or articles. The first three define the branches of government and the powers and limits of each: legislative, executive, and judicial—in that order. The last four get into rules for states to play nicely with each other, the process for making changes to the Constitution, and miscellaneous stuff that doesn't fit anywhere else.

While it may sound intimidating to digest the whole thing, it was initially written on just four sheets of paper. Granted, each sheet was 19 by 37 feet. Just kidding, it's only a little over 4,000 words, not more than a long-winded blog post. We should be thankful that our Constitution's authors were succinct and to the point. India's Constitution is a whopping 117,000 words long, give or take. Our Constitution only has seven articles compared to India's 448. Oh, and if you think 27 amendments is a lot, consider that India has 98 and counting.

With that said, let's get to it.

Here's a bit of trivia that may surprise you. Did you know the Constitution doesn't include the word "democracy?" Not even once. In fact, the word "democratic" isn't in there either.

8

TRANQUILITY, LIBERTY AND FREE STUFF

"We the People of the United States, in Order to form a more perfect Union...."

Famous words, especially the first three, because our government is supposed to be all about us. You know, we, the people. Unlike most other governments, especially the one we whooped during the Revolutionary War, this new one is supposed to be run by the people for the people, just like Honest Abe said.

The preamble specifies the high-level purpose of the Constitution —to define the structure and operation of a new government that will *"establish justice, insure domestic tranquility, provide for the common defense, promote the general welfare, and secure the blessings of liberty to ourselves and our posterity...."*

So that's the reason for the United States Constitution; now, let's see what it says.

Can you spot the typo? While many call out "Pensylvania" as an example of a typo in the original Constitution text, it wasn't. In Article I, Section 2, the spelling seems to be correct, and the state name is written as "Pennsylvania." At the end of the Constitution, where everyone signed, the Keystone State is spelled as "Pensylvania." Technically, that's not a typo, as the single "n" spelling was common for the day. At that time, spelling was more of a guideline than a set of rigid rules. As proof, check out the spelling of Pennsylvania on the Liberty Bell. You guessed it— "Pensylvania."

There's another, which is a legitimate typo, however. In Article I, Section 10, you might spot the word "it's" instead of "its."

9

ARTICLE I: THE LEGISLATIVE BRANCH

Article I must be the most important — because it's the longest, by a country mile. Then again, Article I deals with some heavy stuff, including the structure of Congress, legislative powers of the House of Representatives and the Senate, and the seniority system for Capitol Building parking spots.

The guys who wrote the Constitution did it in priority order, at least regarding power. Article I defines the law-making body—the legislature. As this group would wield the most direct authority in the new government, the founders spent the most time and effort articulating its powers and limitations.

Assistant Clerk to the Pennsylvania General Assembly Jacob Shallus scored the job of penning the Constitution's final draft. He worked at the Pennsylvania State House, also known as Independence Hall, and got approval for the moonlighting job. Word is that he was paid the sum of $30 for his efforts plus seven free promo copies of the Constitution, provided he transcribed them himself. As a state employee, Shallus had easy access to Medicare, which is a good thing as he almost certainly developed a severe case of carpal tunnel syndrome from writing all those pages with an Ostrich feather. How do we know this? Article I has a whopping 2,271 words. By the time Article VII was drafted, the word count *had gone down to 94, and that's including the word "Article" at the beginning.*

While records are unclear, it appears that Shallus didn't actually skewer the sheep on which our country's founding was documented.

Section 1: The Invention of Congress

Section 1 clearly places the blame for all the political bickering squarely at the feet of the founding fathers. Although this section's single sentence uses big words like "vested," all it really says is that legislative powers will be granted to a Congress of the United States.

Just to be clear about the word "legislative," dictionary.com defines the word as "having the function of making laws."

Section 1 also says, *"Congress shall consist of a Senate and House of Representatives."* Apparently, the founders had a serious grudge against future generations because they saddled them with not one group of infantile narcissists but two whole chambers full of them. Thanks, guys.

But seriously, there was deep thinking behind this model. In the minds of the Founding Fathers, while contemplating ideal forms of government, the people that would make laws would be the most powerful (and potentially dangerous) of all. The founders wanted this group to be slow to action, deliberative, and even argumentative. They figured that if a lot of people from different backgrounds were involved in making a joint decision, then there would have to be plenty of compromise along the way. You know, like when the Birtwhistle clan decides to play the question on Family Feud. They huddle, argue, try to persuade each other, and eventually, they tell Steve Harvey their answer. Congress operates the same way, although Family Feud contestants are clearly more efficient.

To ensure that members of Congress never got too cozy with themselves, they created a degree of structural opposition. As we'll see a couple of sections from now, senators were (originally) to be chosen by their state legislatures, while the citizens directly elected representatives in their local communities. The idea was to build in some friction between the two groups having different loyalties.

That's it. So far, this is easy stuff, isn't it?

Are you frustrated at Congress? Does it drive you nuts that the folks responsible for running the country struggle to get along and work together? Well, to a large extent, that's by design. In Federalist 51, Publius (James Madison) explains the importance of creating a balance of power in the most powerful branch of a republican government—the legislature.

"In republican government, the legislative authority necessarily predominates. The remedy for this inconveniency is to divide the legislature into different branches; and to render them, by different modes of election and different principles of action, as little connected with each other as the nature of their common functions and their common dependence on the society will admit."

Section 2: How to Become a Representative

Although Section 2 doesn't specify how frequently congressmen can appear on Sunday morning talk shows, it does outline the structure and makeup of the House of Representatives.

Another annoyance we can blame on the founders is the never-ending onslaught of campaign signs on our local roads. That's because they determined that representatives should be elected every two years. That's to ensure they frequently have to face their constituents and explain their actions.

Have you ever heard a senator accusing a House of Representatives member of kowtowing to the electorate or pandering to voters? For the most part, that's by design. The founders wanted House of Representatives legislators to reflect the current will of the people and be more immediately responsive to their gripes.

The requirements to become a representative are pretty straightforward:

- Must have attained the age of 25 years.
- Must have been a citizen of the United States for seven years.

- Must, when elected, be an inhabitant of that state in which he shall be chosen.

Did you notice that there is no provision barring perpetual liars, perverts, and tax evaders from running for Congress? That explains a lot, doesn't it?

Do you know that census thing that happens every ten years where you're asked all sorts of intrusive questions about your household? That also started here in Section 2. The original purpose was to count free persons and *"those bound to a Service for a Term of Years"* to determine each state's tax contribution and the maximum number of authorized congressional representatives. This is also where that three-fifths of a person rule originated. People who weren't free, otherwise known as slaves, were to count as three-fifths of a free person for terms of the census and, therefore, representation in Congress. We'll return to this topic later, as there's much more to the story.

The original plan was for each state to have at least one representative, but not more than one for every 30,000 people. If you're math inclined, you might notice that we have many more people these days than our number of representatives would indicate.

At the time of this writing, there are about 324 million people in the United States—and that doesn't include the 73 Hollywood actors who have threatened to leave the country if their candidate doesn't win the next election. If there were a representative for each group of 30,000, we would have to start importing interns and press secretaries from China. We'd also have to house the House of Representatives at RFK Stadium because there would be 10,800 Congress Critters all fighting for quality microphone time. If you thought campaign season was annoying now...

Fortunately for the Washington news desks of major television networks, some forward-thinking folks invented the Apportionment Act of 1911. This law permanently limited the number of representatives to 435, arguably about 432 too many, but certainly an improvement over 10,800. Now, as states grow and population shifts, the number of Representatives for each state is determined proportionately by the census, subject to that 435 overall limit.

The power of Impeachment is the other item documented in Section 2, much to former Presidents Andrew Johnson, Bill Clinton, and Donald Trump's chagrin. Kind of like being arrested, Impeachment is just a charge—you can be charged, but you may or may not be found guilty. It's the Senate that sets up a trial to establish ultimate guilt or innocence. As a side note, Johnson, Clinton and Trump were never found guilty by their respective Senates.

As you read this, the number of House of Representatives members is limited to 435. Back in 1789, there were only 65 members, but the House rapidly filled as the country's population grew. By the turn of the 20th Century, things were getting out of control, and some rural areas were nervous about losing influence to more dense population centers. The Apportionment Act of 1911 set a new limit at 435, which has been in place since 1913.

Section 3: How Senators Get Hired... and Fired

Unlike the House of Representatives, where states can send a Volkswagen full of clowns on a road trip to D.C., the Constitution says that each state only gets to send two senators to represent their interests.

According to Section 3 of the Constitution, each senator serves terms of six years before having to go back to the private sector or seek re-election, allowing them to party like rock stars for years at a time before coming back to their home states to face the music.

With the first senatorial class, the founders initiated a staggered system where one-third of the Senate is up for re-election every six years. Since all the first senators started work on the same day, one-third of them drew short straws and only got to collect two years of benefits, and another one-third completed four-year terms. The last third worked a full six years before leaving or seeking re-election.

Since this happens frequently and almost always causes accusations of "that's not constitutional!" we ought to address the provision stated in Section 3 for mid-term appointments. If a serving senator resigns, dies, or is jailed, the state legislature can make a temporary appointment. If the state legislature is not in session, the executive (Governor) can make a temporary appointment.

To become a senator, you must also meet the following criteria.

- You must be 30 or older.
- You must have been a United States Citizen for nine years.
- When elected, you must be a resident of the state you represent.

As Hillary Rodham Clinton showed in 1999, you don't have to be from somewhere to represent it. As a longtime resident of the Great State of Campaigning, Clinton purchased a $1.7 million home in Chappaqua, New York. In November of that year, she officially took up residence, joining the ranks of famous carpetbaggers to run for office in that state.

According to Wikipedia, the modern-day term carpetbagger refers to *"a parachute candidate, an outsider who runs for public office in an area where he or she does not have deep community ties or has lived only for a short time."* It's apparently a New York tradition, with previous carpetbaggers including Robert F. Kennedy and James Buckley. Here's the important takeaway. If you want to become a United States Senator somewhere other than where you live, you only need a lot of money and some serious nerve.

The Constitution also defines the "super-senator," except that person doesn't have power outside of bully pulpit-ing. That would be the Vice President of the United States. The veep can't usually vote but is allowed to attend the meetings. The one time the vice president is allowed to vote is in the event of a hung Senate. Please, insert your own jokes here about hanging the Senate, so I stay out of trouble! But seriously, a hung Senate is where 50 senators disagree, and the other 50 disagree even more. In that event, the vice president gets to cast the deciding vote by calling "infinity plus one!"

Remember the impeachment or arrest power of the House? Well, the senators get to judge all legal proceedings that follow impeachment. In addition to looking stern and speaking to news media about how unpatriotic the offending party is, they get to hear evidence, berate lawyers, and ultimately decide on guilt or innocence. Two-thirds of the present Senate has to agree before someone is deemed guilty. If it happens to be the President of the United States who's getting impeached, then the Chief Justice of the Supreme Court presides over the trial.

While the senators can have a trial to determine whether the impeachment stands, their punishment options are limited. Should you ever get impeached, the Senate can only remove and disqualify you from *"any office of honor, trust, or profit under the United States."* However, don't think you're off the hook from spending time in the slammer. If you did something illegal, the coppers could still arrest, indict, try, judge, and punish you accordingly.

Rules are made to be broken, right? Well, somehow, John Henry Eaton of Tennessee started his United States Senate career at the young age of just 28. No big deal, right? Well, as you now know, the minimum eligibility age for a Senate seat is 30. At that time, ages weren't as well documented as they are now, or perhaps everyone was running the show on the honor system, and we all know how honorable politicians are.

Section 4: Congress Has to Work... On Occasion

My how things have changed. Back in the days when Congress was invented, the idea was that congressmen would hold down regular full-time jobs like the rest of us. When absolutely necessary, they would hop a coach to Washington for a couple of days to take care of government business, then head back to work.

The Constitution only specifies that Congress has to meet once per year, on the first Monday of December, unless they elect to meet on a different day. Did you get that? One day! Modern politicians can't even decide on new curtains for their offices in a single day. Then they've got to worry about muscling the other reps out of the way to get a prime parking space, all the best interns, and first dibs on government-issue Nespresso machines.

Speaking of the day on which festivities officially begin, the 20th

Amendment changed the official start date of the congressional session to January 3rd.

Section 4 also specifies that each state's legislature controls the manner of elections for representatives and senators. However, like most other decisions, Congress has gradually assumed control of that process too. The process of electing senators and representatives was standardized with the 17th Amendment, but we'll get into that later. And as for our current election day, the Tuesday after the first Monday in November? That was established back in 1842.

Most years, Congress is in session about 115 days per year, give or take. That doesn't sound like much, but in fairness, they are expected to split their time between Washington, D.C. and their home districts doing whatever Congress-people do.

Section 5: Thou Shalt Play Nicely With Each Other

Even big kids need rules, and Section 5 establishes the basic ones for representatives and senators.

The first rule is that the majority rules. According to Section 5 of the Constitution, a quorum is required before either group can complete official business. A quorum is defined by half of the members plus one—a simple majority. In practice, this doesn't happen as often as it should, and lots of business is completed with fewer than half the members present. That practice is not as unconstitutional as it may sound, however. Suppose someone present feels strongly that a minority of members shouldn't decide an issue. In that case, they can demand a quorum call, basically saying, "Hey guys, I object to us voting on whether to name the Possum Kingdom, South Carolina Post Office after Miley Cyrus until we have a proper quorum." At that point, the issue has to be tabled until enough members are present for a formal vote on a decision of such great magnitude.

In practice, a quorum call is frequently used as a delaying tactic to postpone votes that opponents aren't too crazy about.

The big rule is that the House and Senate can make their own rules and discipline each other so they can keep their dirty laundry in the family. While the Constitution doesn't go into detail, it allows each house to punish its members for misbehavior. With a two-thirds majority, the house can even expel a really bad apple.

With all the cases of government officials hiding and destroying records, you'd never know the Constitution specifies each house must keep records of its proceedings. While discussions aren't documented, results and decisions are, unless the house agrees it's super-secret. These days, The Congressional Record is published daily. While who votes which way isn't much of a secret anymore, publishing the yes and no votes by name requires the agreement of at least twenty percent of the members present.

Believe it or not, the Senate and House of Representatives are supposed to work with each other, even though they are designed, on purpose, to be independent bodies. To ensure one branch of Congress doesn't take their ball and go home in the event of disagreement, the Constitution prevents either one from adjourning for more than three days if their counterparts are in session unless the other gives permission.

You can always count on politicians to bend the rules to get around these types of restrictions. Both the House and Senate hold pro forma sessions where they are technically "in session," but no business is scheduled. It's kind of like Wal-Mart advertising they're open 7x24, then locking the door and hanging a sign out front that says, "We're open, but you can't actually come in until tomorrow morning when we get here."

In 2014, Wikipedia temporarily banned a range of IP addresses associated with Senate and House of Representatives office computers. Apparently, congressional staffers caused a rash of "fine-tuning" and "polishing" of their bosses' and political adversaries' Wikipedia pages. Consider us shocked.

Section 6: Congressional Benefits

Article I, Section 7 is particularly important to congressmen because it contains the word "emoluments." That means moolah. Compensation. Cash money.

This section solidifies a congressional seat as the greatest job ever. That's because it states that senators and representatives should receive compensation for their services, the rate of which will be ascertained by law. Oh, and guess who makes the laws? That's right! Senators and congressmen make laws that determine their own pay rates. That's a sweet gig.

There's another perk that might be even better for those prone to mouthing off. Senators and representatives are "privileged" from arrest during their time in session and during their travels to and from sessions, which pretty much means all the time. There are exceptions to this immunity for serious charges such as "treason, felony, and breach of the peace."

But seriously, like most things in the Constitution, there's a good reason for these protections, even if they do get abused from time to time. The original idea was to prevent the executive branch—in charge of law enforcement—from harassing members of Congress they don't like. While the president can probably figure out plenty of ways to torment rebellious senators and congressmen, having them arrested on frivolous causes will be tough due to this clause in the Constitution.

Like Super Bowl parties, double dipping is discouraged in Congress too. This section states no one can hold positions in the legislative branch and executive or judicial branches, and vice versa. And while congressmen can vote themselves pay raises, they can't legislate a pay raise for an executive branch job they intend to fill themselves during their term. So if you concoct a nifty plan of creating a new position of Undersecretary of Chuck E. Cheese Skee Ball Tournament Relations with annual compensation of $42,000,357.12 plus a company F-18 fighter jet, you can't take the position yourself, at least until your term is over.

In March 1970, United States Post Office workers in New York and other
cities went on strike to protest wages and working conditions. While not
the sole reason for their angst, part of their frustration arose from their 4%
raise that year while Congress voted itself a 41% increase in pay. President
Nixon called on the National Guard to deliver mail in New York before the
crisis ended.

Section 7: How Bills Are Made

Article I, Section 7 is where the founders discuss the birds and the
bees. You know, how baby bills are made.

To keep this "G" rated, let's just say that the House and Senate
love each other very much, and sometimes, they want to show that by
making a new little bundle of law together. While either one can "be
in the mood" and start the process of getting their bill on, it always
takes both to make a new law. To make this process super awkward,
their father, the president, has to approve of this constitutional copu-
lation, but we'll get into that in a minute.

When making certain types of laws, like those involving taxation
or spending, the House has to initiate the process. The original text of
the Constitution says, "*all bills for raising revenue shall originate in the
House of Representatives.*" Over the years, the House has, as a matter of
practice, taken this to mean bills related to taxation and spending.
Usually, when the Senate gets libidinous about creating their money
bill, the House says, "No, I have a headache," and sends it right back
with something called a blue slip. Over the years, the Senate has
generally tired of this predictable rejection and rarely, if ever, tries to
start a spending bill.

Not left entirely out of the process of raising and spending money,
the Senate can and does change revenue and spending bills initiated
by the House, so they still get to participate in the money-related bill-
making process. And, of course, both chambers have to completely
agree on any type of bill, regardless of whose idea it was.

Once the House and Senate agree on a bill, they send it off to the
President for approval. The President has ten days to consider whether
to approve and sign the new bill. If he agrees, he signs the bill, and it

becomes law. If the president doesn't like the bill, he can veto it, thereby sending it back to whoever came up with the idea in the first place. If the House and Senate want to make a new law over the President's objection, they can overrule the veto with a two-thirds vote.

On the other hand, if the president isn't crazy about approving the bill but doesn't want to be a bully and veto it, he can do one of two things. He can just ignore it for ten days, at which point it becomes law. In this case, he didn't have to sign it, so he can somewhat honestly tell the Sunday morning talk show hosts, "I never supported that legislation!"

The other thing that the president can do is called a pocket veto. If he's lucky on the timing and Congress is not in session, he can hold it for ten days and not return it with a veto because, technically speaking, no one in Congress is at work to receive the vetoed bill. In this case, the bill dies. It's called a pocket veto because the president essentially puts the bill in his pocket forever. It's a nifty political trick that's hard to execute but valuable because a pocket veto can't be overridden—the legislature has to start the process anew.

> When Congress convened for the first time in 1789, the very first official act passed was "An act to regulate the time and manner of administering certain oaths." To be performed by new senators and representatives within three days of taking office, the oath read,
>
> "I, _____, a Representative of the United States in the Congress thereof, do solemnly swear or affirm (as the case may be) that I will support the Constitution of the United States."

Section 8: What Congress Can Do

Is it me, or does it also strike you as funny that Section 8, which outlines the powers of Congress, has the same name as the military regulation used to discharge those unfit for service?

The writers of the Constitution were concerned about limiting the federal government's power. In their view, almost every decision would be better handled locally, at the state, county, or city level. As a result, Article I, Section 8 outlines a specific list of powers that the people voluntarily grant to Congress.

Here's the list of things Congress is allowed to do under the Constitution:

- Tax everyone provided it's for the general welfare of the United States. Early on, there was no individual income tax like we have today. You can thank the 16th Amendment for that little gem. Likewise, it can specify duties and tariffs, provided they're consistent across the United States.
- Borrow money on behalf of the country.
- Regulate commerce between states and internationally.
- Create new citizens! States can't determine the membership rules; only the federal government can.
- Create bankruptcy laws and regulations.
- Print money and decide on how we weigh and measure things. Remember back in the 70s when President Jimmy Carter wanted us to switch to the metric system? Congress said, "Hell, no!" because they're in charge of such "measurement" standardization decisions.
- Congress also gets to decide on a suitable punishment for people who counterfeit money, excluding themselves, of course. They can print all the money they want, penalty-free.
- Create the post office. Ever wonder why you have to stand in line so long at the post office? Because Congress says so, that's why. They also get to decide who gets to be on commemorative stamps.
- Protect the rights of inventors and authors. Property rights were a big deal to the Founding Fathers, and I don't just mean land. If someone thought of a new idea or invention, they felt it essential to protect those property rights. If you're thinking of stealing the design of the Shake Weight and making a billion dollars, forget it. Congress protects

the intellectual property rights of whoever was weird enough to create that product.

- Hire federal judges.
- Punish pirates, presumably by instituting rations on rum.
- Declare war on offending nations.
- Offer pirate licenses for the purpose of plundering enemy vessels. Yeah, we know that two powers ago in this list, Congress was supposed to stop piracy. Still, this provision allows them to offer pirate licenses to anyone who can pass the written, eyesight, and grog drinking exams.
- Hire an army, but only for two years at a time. The Founders were nervous about having a standing army that could decide they wanted to run the country, so they made a rule that forces Congress to re-decide whether to keep issuing paychecks to the troops every two years.
- Hire a navy. Whether the purpose of the Navy was to reign in all those newly minted pirates in training is unclear.
- Hire seasonal help. Congress is also allowed to call up the militia during times of need. The militia means you, me, and Uncle Seamus.
- Create and govern the Emerald City. Section 8 gave Congress the authority to create the nation's capital. Fortunately, Maryland was a compulsive gambler and lost ten square miles of swampland to the feds in a late-night craps game, and the nation's capital was born.
- Build stuff like forts, armories, and Department of Obscure Government Jobs buildings all over the country on land purchased from various state legislatures.
- The Constitution dream team did end Section 8 with a catch-all. That allows Congress to make more laws necessary for carrying out the missions in the previous list and other powers mentioned in the Constitution.

Article I, Section 8 of the Constitution authorizes Congress to issue letters of marque. That's a fancy way of saying they can hire pirates, known as privateers, to raid and capture enemy vessels. A common practice at the time, it hasn't been a matter of United States policy since 1815. However, during the early years of World War II, when a Goodyear blimp flew anti-submarine patrols over the Pacific, some argued that this was a modern use of constitutional power, especially since the blimp's crew was armed with a rifle. If I had worked on that blimp, I totally would have wanted to be known as a pirate.

Section 9: What Congress Can't Do

While Section 8 provides a list of things that Congress can do under the Constitution, Section 9 outlines a list of things that Congress can't do.

Section 9 starts with a passive-aggressive acknowledgment of the slavery dispute. While many assume that all the founders supported slavery, there were more members opposed to it than in support of it.

During the American Revolution and the subsequent early years of our country, it was thought that national unity was essential for survival. Driving a wedge between states over the slavery issue likely would have made the birth of this nation impossible. Without complete unity, victory over King George would be out of reach. Even if possible, the result might have been the birth of multiple independent nations rather than one group of United States. So, under those conditions, slavery might never have been abolished universally. The idea was basically this. *"Let's win this thing; even if we have to punt the slavery issue for a few years, we'll work on that next."*

So, right, wrong, or indifferent, there was a deliberate effort to set aside the debate over slavery for a few years until the nation could stabilize its footing. This first paragraph in Section 9 prohibited Congress from interfering with slave imports until the year 1808 at the earliest. Although, being politicians, they figured out a way to work in a $10 per person tax on the practice. Figures. Those guys can squeeze taxes out of a bag of concrete.

Buried in paragraph 2 is one of the most important concepts that set the new United States apart from so many other forms of government. It prohibits Congress from suspending the privilege of Habeas Corpus except during extreme cases of rebellion or public safety.

What's Habeas Corpus? While the literal translation is something like "you shall have the body," it has nothing to do with promiscuous behavior, although many politicians may beg to differ. What it means is that the government can't imprison, hold or jail you without due process. If the authorities arrest you, they need to declare charges publicly and provide you the opportunity to defend yourself.

The neatest part about Article I, Section 9 is that it's where the word "attainder" shows up. What's an attainder? Think of a bill of attainder this way. Suppose Congress decided to vote into law a bill that says people who have covered themselves with Spam and roller skated through the National Mall are guilty of general grossness and have to go immediately to jail without trial. Since the "law" avoids the legal system and process, it would be considered a bill of attainder. In general terms, Congress can't make a law that immediately classifies a person or group of people as guilty.

Similarly, Congress has to provide advance notice of things that are going to be considered bad behavior. If they want to decide that watching 19 straight hours of The Kardashians should be illegal, not to mention a colossal waste of time, they have to pass the law first before people can be prosecuted. And even then, you're entitled to argue your case in front of Judge Judy.

Back before the national individual income tax, states would make contributions to the federal government. Section 9 specifies that any levies like this need to be in proportion to the population of each state. It would be unfair to tax Rhode Island $94 billion while New York only kicks in $9.95, a dozen cannolis, and an all-expenses-paid weekend with Times Square Elmo.

Also, to support fairness between the states, Congress can't charge duties on goods moving between states or coming into specific states. Congress can't make policies that make it more favorable for international trade to occur in one state versus another. It's just like moms and dads with more than one child. "We love you all the same!" Since the early southern states depended heavily on exports of things like cotton, tobacco, and guitar rock, the Constitution also forbade Congress from taxing exports.

Buried in clause seven is one of the most important concepts in all of Article I. It states that Congress is in charge of the national pocketbook—no exceptions. Not even the president can spend one dime of public money without approval from Congress, at least technically speaking. Likewise, Congress is also responsible for showing us periodic statements of receipts and expenditures. However, they've handily surpassed the average married person's skills when hiding inappropriate spending habits.

With the exception of Hollywood entertainers and sports icons, there shall be no nobility in the United States. Congress can't bestow titles like King, Duke, and Baroness on citizens, not counting, of course, the Kardashians. Government employees and elected officials also can't accept titles or even gifts from other countries without the explicit permission of Congress.

According to an International Business Times article published in 2011, 30 major corporations spent more money between 2008 and 2010 lobbying members of Congress to get their way than they paid in income taxes. During those three years, these companies racked up schmoozing expenses of over $400,000 per day—and that included weekends.

Section 10: Limits on State Powers

Section 10 lays down the law, at least partly, for proper state behavior. While the Constitution goes to great lengths to preserve independence and power at the state level, some things are better handled centrally. You know, like air conditioning.

In short, Section 10 prohibits states from entering into their own treaties. So, for example, even though there's a booming French restaurant business in New Orleans, the state of Louisiana can't make a treaty with France prohibiting imports of Gruyere cheese to New Jersey.

Remember in Section 8 where Congress can grant provisional pirate's licenses? Well, states can't do that, not even Florida.

Since the Constitution prohibits Congress from doing certain bad things, the framers thought it a good idea to clarify that the states can't do those same bad things on their own. As a result, states can't print their own money, pass bills of attainder, or grant titles of nobility.

States lucky enough to have purchased waterfront property while it was still affordable can't charge their own import duties. While it would be a significant revenue opportunity, it wouldn't be considered fair to states like South Dakota, which were too late for the ocean-front property auction.

Last but not least, states aren't allowed to run their own wars on land or sea; that's reserved for the federal government and sneaky presidents.

As we write this, there are rumblings from California about some residents wanting to secede from the United States. It's not a new topic. That whole secession idea started back in the Civil War. And many residents of the State of Texas have long believed that the state has a "right" to secede from the union because it was its own republic for nine years before joining as a state. Constitutionally, that doesn't fly because when a state joins the union, they agree to an indissoluble arrangement. Supreme Court Justice Antonin Scalia summed it up this way. "If there was any constitutional issue resolved by the Civil War, it is that there is no right to secede."

10

ARTICLE II: THE EXECUTIVE BRANCH

If you want to know whether a president is acting constitutionally or not, ignore the blathering on cable talk shows and refer to Article II.

While Article I outlines the definition, role, and powers of Congress, Article II defines the role of the head of the executive branch of government—The President. It describes the selection process of the Commander-in-Chief, his or her authority and powers, and even the verbiage of the president's oath.

In the ultimate and final act of patriotism, three different United States presidents died on July 4—Independence Day. Thomas Jefferson and John Adams died less than six hours apart on July 4, 1826, although we don't think they planned that maneuver. Jefferson was keen on making it to the 50th Anniversary of the Declaration of Independence. He did. James Monroe died on July 4, 1831.

Section 1: How to Become President

Here's the bottom line: If you get elected president, you can live in the big house on Pennsylvania Avenue for at least four years unless you get into trouble, as outlined in Section 4. While you don't have to share the mansion with your Vice President, that person is chosen for the same term.

If you've been baffled by the presidential primary processes of each state, there's a reason for that. According to Section 1, each state can decide how to choose its electors, who collectively cast votes for the president. This was one of those compromises reached during the arguments over the Constitution itself. Some people wanted a direct popular vote. Others wanted Congress to choose the president. This whole idea of electors was intended to give each state an "equal say" in the presidential elections, even though some states are more populous than others.

This is a great place to pause for an explanation of this whole electoral system. It frustrates us today, probably because we have zero attention span, but if you stop to think about the rationale behind it, the electoral system makes sense.

The best explanation of the electoral college I've heard was from former Texas State Representative, attorney, and constitutional speaker Rick Green. He explains the reasoning for the electoral system by comparing it to America's favorite pastime—baseball. The guy who invented the World Series decided that the World Champions should be the team that played the best over a series of games, in different cities, and with different players rotated in and out of the games throughout the series. The champion should be the team that plays the best overall, under different circumstances.

Suppose for a minute the winner of the World Series was the team that scored the most runs over seven games. That sounds logical, right? Well, maybe not. In 1960, the Pittsburgh Pirates won the World Series over the New York Yankees four games to three. Strangely enough, the Yankees scored 55 runs during the series, but the Pirates only scored 27. The Yankees should have won, right? Nope, because the Pirates won four games. Matching up against different pitchers, on different nights, in different parks, the Pirates played a better overall series and became the champs. Just because, during a couple of the games, the Yankees lit up a pitcher or two and ran up the score, should they have won the series? I don't think so. This scenario happens in baseball playoff and World Series situations about 15 percent of the time.

The electoral college works on the same theory, which is why the founders created this model in the first place. If the president were determined by the raw number of popular votes nationwide, then the most populated areas would determine the winner every four years. We'd have to change the job title to "President of the United States of California." No candidate would ever spend 30 seconds campaigning in any state other than the three or four most populous ones so that the minority states would have no real say in the process.

The founders believed a president must appeal to citizens throughout the nation, not just those in a handful of large cities. The more well-rounded the presidential candidate, the better for all. The founders recognized that every locale was different, and citizens of each had different desires, goals, and priorities. That's one of the reasons that there is such an emphasis on local representation at the state level.

So that's the side story of the electoral system.

Section 1 dictates that the number of electors for each state will be limited to the number of senators plus the number of representatives, but there's no double dipping. In other words, if you're a senator or representative, you cannot, by the decree of this section of the Constitution, be an elector. You can influence, fundraise, cajole, threaten, and beg, but you can't cast an electoral vote in a presidential election.

As originally outlined by the Constitution, the process of picking the president was a little different than what we know today. Since electronic ballot machines had yet to be invented, each elector wrote down a vote for two individuals they thought would make swell presidents. At the state level, the votes would be tallied for all that state's electors and the sealed list was sent to the President of the Senate. In the presence of the Senate and House of Representatives members, the Senate President opened the sealed ballot counts from each state and awarded the White House keys to the person who got a majority vote. In the event of a tie, the House of Representatives would immediately vote to determine the winner. If no one was popular enough to obtain a majority of the electors, then the top five went into a vote by the House of Representatives. However, instead of each representative getting one vote, each state got one vote. A majority was still required, and two-thirds of states must vote. In this scenario, the vice president was the second highest vote getter. If there was a tie for second place, the Senate had to vote on the veep pick. Got all that? Good, because it all changed with the 12th Amendment.

Apparently, the election of 1800 under this system was even more of a nightmare than modern presidential elections, so we changed the rules completely. Never fear, though; we still have a popular vote and an electoral system to keep things plenty confusing.

So, the original method of choosing a president was exceedingly complex. Fortunately, the following clause is simple. Congress gets to decide the date of the presidential election. For 150 years or so, it's been the Tuesday after the first Monday in November.

Not to step into a can of worms here, but this section also specifies that the president must be a "natural-born citizen, or a citizen of the United States, at the time of the adoption of this Constitution."

The gotcha is the Constitution never defines what precisely a "natural-born citizen" is. Based on how jolly old England handled the matter, the prevailing sentiment is that anyone born to United States citizens, regardless of where the parents happen to be at the time, is a natural-born citizen.

If mom U.S. Citizen and dad U.S. Citizen plan a trip to Barbados for a bit of sun and fun, and baby U.S. Citizen happens to fall out while in that country, then that child is generally assumed to be a natural-born citizen. Another way to look at the matter is, does the person have to go through some naturalization process to become a citizen? It's a question that will never be solved until Congress weighs in with some clarity. As if that'll ever happen.

Presidents also must have survived that youthful and irresponsible stage and reached the ripe old age of 35. This section of the Constitution also states that the president must have been a resident within the United States for fourteen years.

In the original Constitution, responsibilities were passed to the vice president if something happened to the president, like resignation, death, or some other inability to perform the duties. If something happened to both, Congress chose someone to act as president until a new president was elected. This was changed quite a bit with the ratification of the 25th Amendment, but we'll get to that later.

Guess what? If you're elected president, you'll get paid! And to prevent political spats between Congress and the president, Article II, Section 1 states that Congress can't give the president a pay raise or a pay cut while that person is in office. As much as Congress may want to reduce the presidential salary to $14 and cancel the company jet, they can't. The president also can't moonlight to make money doing other things for the federal government or the states' governments.

Last but not least, every president has to say the following and mean it:

> *"I do solemnly swear (or affirm) that I will faithfully execute the Office of President of the United States and will to the best of my ability, preserve, protect and defend the Constitution of the United States."*

Want to stump your friends and win a serious bar bet? Ask them this question: Who was the first president born in the United States?

The answer? The 8th president, Martin Van Buren. Sure, all of his predecessors were born in places like Massachusetts, Virginia, and South Carolina, but that was before the United States was a country. So, Van Buren was the first born a United States citizen.

For extra points, you can toss in the fact that he's credited with "inventing" the saying, "OK." His birthplace of Kinderhook, New York, was also known as "Old Kinderhook." Social gatherings took on the "Old Kinderhook" name, and one thing led to another until the initials OK came to mean that everything is hunky dory.

Section 2: Presidential Powers

According to Section 2, the president is the boss of the executive branch of the federal government. That means he or she is the Commander-in-Chief of the armed forces and any state national guard units that have been called for federal service. The president is also in charge of the federal agencies and departments in the executive branch.

One power that's especially popular with large campaign donors and Wall Street financiers is the presidential pardon. Not counting impeachments of government officials, the president can pardon anyone they choose (read: big donors) of any federal crime.

Planning cocktail parties with other countries is a presidential duty. However, if it's serious, as with a binding treaty, the Senate has to agree with a two-thirds majority vote, or the agreement is null and void.

While Article I of the Constitution prohibits Congress from bestowing titles of nobility to United States citizens, nothing in there prevents a city from being named after a president. The capital of Liberia, Monrovia, was named after President James Monroe in honor of his support of the colonization of that country.

Not only does the president get to pick the wallpaper in the East Wing guest bathroom, but he also gets to hire a bunch of folks. However, these "nominations" require the "advice and consent" of the Senate, which means a simple majority vote approval. For example, the president chooses ambassadors to other countries, Supreme Court justices, federal judges, cabinet members, agency chiefs, and other officers where the Constitution does not explicitly define the selection process.

One exception to the need for Senate approval is a recess appointment. While the Senate is out of session, the president can fill vacant job positions without explicit Senate approval, at least temporarily. Positions filled with recess appointments like this are only valid until the end of the next Senate session, which basically means that the Senate can undo the president's selection if they so desire.

Section 3: Presidential Miscellany

One underlying theme of everything in the Constitution is the mistrust of authority. The founders designed this system of checks and balances to keep anyone in government from getting a big head about their power and influence. The president wasn't above this mistrust, and Section 3 calls for a report to Congress on the State of the Union "from time to time."

In the event of national emergencies, as determined by the president, he or she can call both houses of Congress into session (if they're not already) to address national business. An interesting "power" granted in Section 3 also allows the president to adjourn Congress.

Those extravagant state dinners we see on TV are approved in Section 3 as the president is granted authority to "receive Ambassadors and other public ministers."

The president must also faithfully execute the laws of the nation as defined by Congress.

The president is also responsible for commissioning officers of the United States military, although this is not generally done personally. Can you imagine the line of fresh-faced Second Lieutenants waiting to get tapped on each shoulder with a gleaming sword?

George Washington's salary for serving as President of the United States was $25,000. John Adams, filling the role of vice president, earned $5,000 per year. The presidency became a six-figure job in 1949 when Harry Truman earned a cool $100,000 plus an additional $50,000 non-taxable expense account. Now, the president earns $400,000 annually but has plenty of sweet perks like unlimited rides on Air Force One while in office.

Section 4: Presidential Discipline

The final section of Article II says the president, vice president, and everyone who works for them better well behave, or else there could be a timeout imposed by Congress. Congress retains the power to impeach and remove from office anyone who is convicted of treason, bribery, or "other high crimes and misdemeanors."

We've heard a lot about impeaching over the years, and three presidents have actually been impeached, Andrew Johnson, Bill Clinton and Donald Trump. Richard Nixon was a close runner-up, but he resigned before Congress finished impeachment proceedings. But what does impeachment mean? It's kind of like the process you hear about in every episode of Law and Order—indictment. It's an accusation, or leveling of charges, against an official. It's not a trial, conviction, or even evidence of guilt. That has to be established by the Senate. To date, no president has ever been removed from office due to impeachment and conviction. I'm confident they'll keep trying.

While it didn't cause impeachment, President Warren Harding had the reputation of being somewhat the gambler. His "Poker Cabinet" was reportedly quite the regular social event, complete with plenty of bootleg liquor during the Prohibition years. On one occasion, he bet a set of White House china on a hand—and lost.

11

ARTICLE III: THE JUDICIAL BRANCH

If you've been paying attention to civics class, you'll probably guess what Article III of the Constitution covers. Article I defined the legislative branch of government. Article II defined the executive branch. Article III defines the duties of the judicial branch.

If you look at the original text of the Constitution later in this book, you'll see that Article III is the shortest of the first three articles. That's deliberate and reflects the level of power of the judicial branch. The judicial branch exists to apply the law made by the legislative branch and implemented by the executive branch—that's it. Whichever side of the political aisle you're on, legislating from the bench is most unconstitutional, as we're about to see.

Article III established the Supreme Court and federal court system but left the details to Congress. The Judiciary Act of 1789, technically known as An Act to Establish the Judicial Courts of the United States, established the structure of the federal court system and created the position of Attorney General. President George Washington signed it into law on September 24, 1789.

Section 1: The Supremes

Stop! In the name of justice, because ain't no mountain higher than the Supreme Court, and Article III, Section 1 says so. Nor can you hurry justice; you'll just have to wait because justice don't come easy; it's a game of give and take.

Section 1 also establishes inferior courts, the number and structure of which are to be determined by Congress. After all, the Supreme Court can't hear every case, so the system is built like a hierarchy. Cases are heard and decided locally, with local jury oversight. If things are unclear, cases are pushed up the ladder to higher courts. If it's a really tough one for both sides, someday, they'll be together... at the Supreme Court. This court is the head of the entire judicial branch of the federal government, so if the Chief Justice says, "Come see about me," then you've gone as far as you can go.

This section of the Constitution also dictates that judges are nominated for life positions, the idea being to remove them from the whims of political winds. Not having to worry about re-election means less incentive to react to the political pressures of the day. No matter who is in office, in theory, at least, they can't exert influence over the courts. For the same reason, Congress is also prevented from mucking around with a justice's salary while they are in office.

Each year, about 8,000 cases are filed with the Supreme Court. Clearly, the nine justices can't deal with that sort of volume, especially considering the level of depth of each case. If lower courts can't sort the issues out, you can bet these cases are complicated. The Supreme Court grants plenary review, complete with oral arguments by attorneys, in only about 80 cases per year. That's not surprising considering that each of these cases generates thousands of pages of supporting documents and written opinions.

Section 2: Supremely in Charge of What?

Section 2 defines the scope of the Supreme Court's authority. First, the court has the final say over cases involving issues explicitly defined by the Constitution. Additionally, the court is responsible for international cases involving treaties, ambassadors, and other public ministers. The court also has authority over conflicts between states, residents of different states, and individuals and states. We'll get to the specifics of said authority in a minute.

First, we have to talk about a really big deal raised by a prospective Justice of the Peace for Washington, D.C., William Marbury. Hang on to your shorts, this gets a bit complicated, and the story could fill an entire book. We'll touch on the highlights here because the case raised an issue of great constitutional importance, as you'll soon see.

It's 1801. Thomas Jefferson had just been elected president but hadn't yet taken office. The outgoing head honcho was John Adams, a raging Federalist. He wanted to tweak Jefferson and the incoming administration, so he and Congress created a bunch of new courts that Adams could fill with officials he liked.

Adams selected dozens of new federalist judges during the last hours (literally) of his presidency to stack the courts with like-minded people before Jefferson could fill the courts with rabid Anti-Federalists. Most of the new justices received their appointment commissions while Adams was still in charge. But, if the commission didn't physically arrive, then the appointment was not yet active, and the judge couldn't do the judge thing. So far, so good?

Anyway, Marbury did not get his commission before Jefferson took the oath as the new president. Since Adams peeved Jefferson by adding all these new judges, Jefferson said something to the effect of, "Ummm, dude, I ain't gonna commission the rest of your judges."

Adams and Marbury are ticked. In their mind, Marbury is a certified Justice of the Peace because he's been properly appointed and approved—it's only the paperwork that hasn't yet arrived via United Pony Service.

Marbury says, "Fine. I'm suing all y'all," and proceeds to file his case directly with the Supremes. Remember this—he filed directly with the Supreme Court. This detail turns out to be important later.

Article III, Section 2 states the types of cases where the Supreme Court has direct authority and where it has appellate authority. In other words, for cases like international disputes and disputes involving a state as one of the parties, one can call 1-800-SUP-REME and get on the docket to get the case heard. For other types of cases, like those covered by state law or involving individuals in a state, the only way it can get to the Supreme Court is through the appeals process. The sue-ers and sue-ees have to file locally, then appeal their way up to the Supreme Court.

OK, now back to Marbury. His goal was to encourage the court to force Jefferson's administration to deliver his commission so he could get busy judging things. He wanted the court to issue what's called a writ of mandamus. That's a fancy word for a court order telling someone to do something. Some years earlier, Congress had passed the Judiciary Act of 1789. One of its provisions (at least in the view of the justices involved in this case) was what allowed Marbury to file his case directly with the Supreme Court and ask for the remedy of a writ of mandamus.

The Supreme Court agreed with Marbury and ruled that he had been wronged, and he should be able to get the situation corrected. However, and most importantly, the Supremes said, "Yo, it's not our problem, and we don't have the authority to fix it anyway. In fact, we don't even have the authority to hear this case."

The court said that the Judiciary Act of 1789 was unconstitutional in the first place. Hence, the congressionally created provision that allowed Marbury to file directly to the Supreme Court was invalid. As a result, they couldn't hear the case, and Marbury had to figure out another way to seek justice.

The moral of the story? Being right doesn't necessarily mean you win. But more importantly, in constitutional terms, the Court put its collective foot down and said it had the authority to determine whether laws passed by Congress were constitutional. If Congress were to pass an unconstitutional law, like the Judiciary Act of 1789 (in their view), then the Supreme Court had the power to declare it invalid.

This was a really, really big deal, mainly because the Constitution never says explicitly who has the power over a law that may be unconstitutional. Congress makes laws, but does that give them the authority to make a law that violates the Constitution? Or can the

Supreme Court perform judicial review of laws so that they may strike them down if they violate the intent of the Constitution?

The case was a mess, then and now, as all sorts of weird factors muddied the waters. Some say that Chief Justice John Marshall should never have been involved in the case because he was also acting as Secretary of State at the time and had a conflict of interest. Others claim that the Supreme Court did have direct jurisdiction to issue the writ because the case arguably involved "public ministers and consuls," as worded in Article III, Section 2. Regardless, the case planted a stake in the ground that claimed the court has the authority of judicial review over laws passed by Congress.

Last but not least, in Section 2, with the exception of impeachments, which Congress handles, those accused of crimes are entitled to a trial by jury, which must take place in the state where the crime was committed.

The Supreme Court didn't hear a single case during its first year of existence. Not because everyone agreed on everything but because that time was spent architecting the day-to-day operations of the brand spanking new federal legal system. The court heard its first case (Van Staphorst v. Maryland) in year two and handed down its first opinion on August 3, 1791, in the case of West v. Barnes. That case dealt with a farm mortgage dispute. West, the farmer, lost on procedural grounds. Something about a writ being signed and sealed by a Rhode Island clerk rather than the Supreme Court clerk. Ah, technicalities...

Section 3: Treasonous Traitors

Like most things covered in the Constitution, there's much more to the story of Article III, Section 3 than meets the eye. This section calls out the issue of treason against the United States. Interestingly, treason is the only crime specifically defined in the Constitution.

First, treason is defined as actively going to war against the United States or aiding and abetting the enemies of the United States. I believe the wording "*Treason against the United States, shall consist only in levying war against... etc.*" also serves a deeper purpose. By calling out the limitations to acts that can be defined as treason, they also identify many things that aren't treason. In other words, the Founders did this to prevent bad apples from using treason charges as political weapons. Disagreement and nasty accusations are fine (legally in this case) if not respectful and don't define treason. The First Amendment, which we'll discuss later, offers additional protection for dissenting opinions.

Additionally, a specific burden of proof for the crime of treason is specified. Two witnesses to the specific act of treason must testify in court, or the suspect must openly confess to the crime.

Last but not least, Section 3 allows Congress to specify punishments for the crime of treason but prevents them from applying punishment or harm to relatives of the traitor.

The Supreme Court is nothing, if not full of fascinating traditions. While justices don't wear those big, fluffy wigs anymore—that only happened once before the wearer was taunted to the point of dumping the curls— they do honor some other long-standing practices. Each day, white quill pens are placed at desks when the court is sitting. For many years, formal dress was expected and required—morning coats only. Today, Department of Justice lawyers continue the traditional dress custom. While opinions may vary, respect is paramount; each justice shakes hands with every other at the beginning of bench and conference sessions. One tradition missed by no one is the requirement to go on the road. For over 100 years, the Supreme Court Justices would have to hold court in each circuit across the country. When travel was limited to horse and buggy, that was a grueling routine.

12

ARTICLE IV: STATE RELATIONS

Article IV spells out the rules about how states have to play nicely with each other and the federal government.

Section 1: Mutual Respect of States

At first glance, Article IV, Section 1 seems to make no sense whatsoever.

> *"Full Faith and Credit shall be given in each State to the public Acts, Records, and judicial Proceedings of every other State. And the Congress may by general Laws prescribe the Manner in which such Acts, Records, and Proceedings shall be proved, and the Effect thereof."*

Got that? If you didn't, that's OK because it reads like gibberish to most other people too. Let's see if we can put this one into language that even a politician can understand.

Each state has to recognize official stuff like laws, records, and licenses from other states.

Like most things, it's not quite that simple. States don't have to agree with or adhere to every law passed in any other state. Just because California mandates that every citizen spends 317 hours per year surfing doesn't mean that Minnesotans are obligated to do the same. Even licenses aren't so simple. If I acquire a Hamster Cosmetology license in Missouri, I'll most likely need to get a new one should I move to Indiana.

Historically, this clause has been called on to protect judgment issues more than public policy ones. The Supreme Court has supported states' authority to enact and enforce public policy decisions, provided that said decisions don't violate constitutional rights. Even the 2015 Supreme Court decision in Obergefell v. Hodges that held for a fundamental right to same-sex marriage didn't rely on Article IV. That decision referenced the 14th Amendment, but we'll get to that later.

Things can get messy under Article IV, Section 1 pretty quickly in the face of contradictory laws. That's why this section ends by authorizing Congress to define to what degree states must recognize each other's laws.

While clauses in the 27 constitutional amendments alter, change, and even remove content from the original Constitution, creating and ratifying an amendment that cancels out a previous amendment seems a bit wishy-washy, doesn't it? That's precisely what happened with the 21st Amendment. It nullified the 18th Amendment, so we can now enjoy a beer at ball games again.

Section 2: Crime and State Lines

Right off the bat, Section 2 prohibits discrimination against citizens of other states, even if you really hate their football team. Say you live in South Carolina, and you're driving through Alabama to watch the Clemson Tigers play. Being anxious to get the wings on the grill at the upcoming tailgate party, you're going a little too fast. While you can get a whopper of a speeding ticket from Officer Crimson Tide, take comfort in the knowledge that your new roadside velocity enforcement buddy can't write the same ticket at a reduced rate for Alabama fans, at least not legally.

This is also the part of the Constitution that defines extradition. If I buy a Bugatti Veyron in Montana and some other evil Montanan steals it, I'll obviously have legal recourse in a Montana court of law, and that car rustling weasel will face criminal charges if caught. In part, thanks to Article IV, Section 1, if that guy drives across the state line into Idaho and gets arrested there, he has to be sent back to Montana to face the music for swiping my wheels. You can run, but you can't hide from the state where you committed a crime — at least not in another state.

While not directly stated within the text, this section is instrumental in defining the freedom with which Americans can cross state lines. If you want to drive to Georgia to have breakfast at Cracker Barrel, you go right on ahead. No permits, papers, or visas are required, and the extra side of bacon is priced quite reasonably. By the way, their sweet tea is excellent.

Section 2 closes with some serious verbal tap dancing. The whole idea of slavery was a hotly contested issue during the creation of the Constitution. Most founders were vigorously opposed to it, while some remained in favor. Knowing that the issue was an abrupt deal breaker for any hope of national unity, those in the know allowed clauses like this one, realizing that if they played their cards right, they could solve the slavery issue at a later date.

> *"No Person held to Service or Labour in one State, under the Laws thereof, escaping into another, shall, in Consequence of any Law or Regulation therein, be discharged from such Service or Labour, but shall be delivered up on Claim of the Party to whom such Service or Labour may be due."*

This section is commonly known as the fugitive slave clause. Notice that there is no use of the word "slave" but rather the description "person held to Service or Labour." Regardless of the wording, this section required that slaves who escaped to free states must be returned to their owners, regardless of any anti-slavery laws present in the free state. This clause was later nullified by the 13th Amendment, which abolished slavery altogether.

Section 3: New States?

If you want to develop your very own state, you've got to abide by the rules of Article IV, Section 3. The admission clause specifies that Congress has the authority to add new states, but with some provisions. In fact, 37 new states have been added since the writing of Article IV, Section 3. You may have noticed that all those newly adopted states inherited the same footing and benefits as the original natural-born 13. Equal treatment for new states isn't spelled out explicitly in this section but has become a matter of practice.

More specifically, Section 3 says ixnay to the concept of marriage between states. If California wanted to join forces with Oregon (Californegon), the Virginia's decided to tag team (West Virginia Virginia), or maybe Mississippi launched a takeover bid on Alabama (MissAlabama), the plan would be prohibited. Along the same lines, states can't subdivide like amoebas, nor can Congress subdivide states. This section is silent on the issue of a state deciding to bail out of the union, although the Supreme Court has ruled that statehood is an indissoluble agreement.

Section three also speaks to congressional authority over territories and properties owned by the United States. While this refers to lands like Puerto Rico and Guam, it also comes into play for federally owned property within various states. For example, the federal government owns and controls the vast majority of the state of Nevada, so the folks in Washington control most of that state, at least in terms of geography.

While hard facts are sketchy on this one, as the constitutional lore goes, one delegate suggested that the standing army of the new United States be limited to 5,000 troops. According to the legend, George Washington offered a somewhat sarcastic response, agreeing with this proposal provided that the Constitution also limited the size of any future invading armies to 3,000 men. Whether true or not, it makes for a great story, doesn't it?

Section 4: State Government Behavior

The Constitution as a whole defines and implicitly protects all citizens by organizing a form of republican government. Remember, that doesn't refer to a political party but rather a form of government where citizens hold power and call the shots, usually through some representation model. The first clause of Section 4 places the requirement of having a "Republican Form of Government" in each state as well. This clause doesn't define the exact structure that state governments need to assume but rather implicitly points to the remainder of the Constitution to define the principles that must be followed. If Hollywood wants to crown the Academy Awards Best Supporting Actors as King and Queen of the state of California, that won't fly, at least not in a legally binding sense.

If you're losing sleep at night worrying about whether France will try to seize Louisiana or the Norwegians will invade Minnesota, rest easy. Section 4 guarantees that the rest of the union will come to the rescue. Granted, neither warrants much of a threat, but it's still comforting, isn't it? A similar guarantee exists to protect against domestic violence or insurrection in any state. The bottom line? As part of a union, states are to help each other out in times of need.

The "Rogue Island" was not all that keen on the new Constitution. In at least one public vote on ratification, 92% of voters pulled the lever against ratification.

13

ARTICLE V: HOW TO CHANGE THE RULES

The folks who hashed out the constitution were smart enough to know a single document couldn't define every possible decision and eventuality for all time. That's part of the reason so much thought, effort, and squabbling went into the structure of government. With a good structure that supports founding principles, decisions can be made over time as required that are consistent with the protection of liberty. Even still, the founders foresaw the need to amend the terms of the original Constitution over time, so they designed a process for that and documented it in Article V.

Two things must happen to amend the Constitution. First, someone must draft the text of a proposed amendment. Next, the existing states must ratify that proposed change before it can be printed in all those pocket Constitution handbooks.

There are two ways amendments can be proposed. First, two-thirds of both the House and Senate can propose an amendment. Since two-thirds of Congress can't agree on whether the congressional cafeteria should still serve Tab diet soda, there's another way. Two-thirds of the state legislatures can call for a Constitutional Convention where amendments can be proposed.

The second part of the process is ratification. Proposed changes are just that—proposed—until three-quarters of the states agree to the new measures. Congress can specify whether ratification will occur via state legislatures or special state ratification conventions.

Since this all started, there have been over 11,000 proposed changes, with just 33 constitutional amendments sent for ratification. Only 27 have been approved by the required number of states—the original ten in the Bill of Rights and 17 others over time.

Some proposed changes probably sound familiar. While many states have adopted balanced budget amendments to their constitutions, the federal government has not, even though the proposal has come up several times. Successful proposal and ratification of the 22nd Amendment implemented term limits for the office of president, but no such amendments for congressional term limits have completed the process. Shockingly, a proposed amendment docking the pay of legislators for each day they fail to come up with a budget died on the vine.

Article V provides a great example of some early wheeling and dealing. At risk of grossly oversimplifying the slavery issue, the thinking went something like this:

- Many of the founders were opposed to slavery at the time that the Constitution was negotiated and drafted.
- Those opposed were not in a position to demand that slavery be banned within the terms of the Constitution because some of their counterparts, representing slave states, never would have joined the union.
- For reasons discussed earlier in this book, the most important thing was establishing a "powerful enough" union of states. That was seen as the only practical way to protect the country, states, and individual liberties.
- Anti-slavery advocates figured they could address the slavery problem after the successful creation of the country with the proper governmental structure.
- Slavery advocates wanted to prevent folks from immediately abolishing slavery upon ratification of the Constitution.

- In typical Washington form, the solution was to kick the can down the road and let future legislators deal with it. That's why Article I, Section 9 specifically prohibits Congress from passing any law prohibiting the importation of slaves before 1808.

And that's why Article V specifically shields certain parts of Article I, Section 9 from constitutional amendments before 1808.

Scholars have debated at length about alternate ways to "change" the Constitution. Certainly, as the ultimate arbiter of what the Constitution really says, the Supreme Court has the power (in a practical if not constitutional sense) to "adjust" the meaning of the Constitution. They can't change the words, but they can and do weigh in on what those words really mean—right, wrong or indifferent.

Academics also suggest that the Constitution itself is, in part, designed to ensure that the inertia of government never suppresses the will of the people. The people always have the right to make a direct change, with or without the Article V process. How exactly that would look is unspecified. In our view, it's largely irrelevant, as our system is designed from the ground up on a foundation of voluntary consent. The rules only work if most people continue to agree to follow the rules for the common good.

One of the more interesting proposed constitutional changes came from Wisconsin Representative Victor Berger in 1922. Keeping in mind that Berger was a House of Representatives member, he proposed to abolish the United States Senate. You can sense his frustration from the preamble to his proposed constitutional amendment. "Whereas the Senate in particular has become an obstructive and useless body, a menace to the liberties of the people, and an obstacle to social growth; a body, many of the Members of which are representatives neither of a State nor of its people, but solely of certain predatory combinations, and a body which, by reason of the corruption often attending the election of its Members, has furnished the gravest public scandals in the history of the nation...."

14

ARTICLE VI: CONSTITUTIONAL SUPREMACY

Article VI includes three clauses that imply that the buck stops with the feds.

The first clause guarantees that the new United States government would assume all previous debts and responsibilities entered into before the adoption of the Constitution. More specifically, any agreements agreed to under the Articles of Confederation would be honored as before.

Second, the Supremacy Clause takes us smack into the nuances of federalism. In this constitutional republic, the federal government and states share power, with the constitution specifically enumerating situations where states (and technically individuals) cede authority to the federal government.

For example, all state legislators, officers, and judges would be bound to the national treaties and laws stemming from the Constitution. The purpose of this clause was to prevent conflicting legal principles between state and federal governments. To be clear, all authority not explicitly assigned to the federal government via the constitution remains close to the people at the state level. The supremacy clause addresses the potential conflict between federal and state law.

As a simple example, no state can pass a law denying women the right to vote as that is a constitutionally protected right defined by the 19th Amendment.

To make this federal supremacy rule clear to state officers, Article VI requires an oath to the Constitution. Congress can specify the details of that oath, but, you guessed it, it has to be constitutional.

Since the Constitutional Convention proceedings were secret, no one outside saw the results until September 19, 1787, when John Dunlap and David Claypoole printed a version of it in the Pennsylvania Packet and Daily Advertiser.

15

ARTICLE VII: CONSTITUTIONAL RATIFICATION

Wouldn't it be hypocritical if the guys who wrote this Constitution rammed it down everyone else's throats? They recognized that risk, and Article VII specifies that none of this was valid unless nine states ratified it first.

At the time, there were 13 states, which translated to 69.23076923 percent of states needing to approve the adoption of the Constitution. You might recall that Article V specifies that three-quarters of states are required to ratify changes to the Constitution. Why the difference? Most likely because of rounding error. If the framers had required ten states instead of nine, that would have worked out to 76.92307692 percent. That and the likely worry over the coming ratification fight. The more you know.

When the Constitution was signed, the population of the new United States was about four million. Since then, we've churned out an additional 320 million new citizens, give or take.

16

THE BILL OF RIGHTS

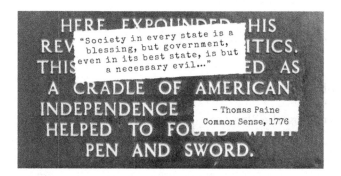

HERE EXPOUNDED HIS
REV ITICS.
THIS D AS
A CRADLE OF AMERICAN
INDEPENDENCE
HELPED TO FO
PEN AND SWORD.

"Society in every state is a blessing, but government, even in its best state, is but a necessary evil..."

– Thomas Paine
Common Sense, 1776

The First Constitutional Changes

How quickly we forget.

When the Constitution was drafted, debated, and ratified, the people involved had just been through an insulting experience, at least regarding natural rights violations, so important underlying concepts like the following were right in the forefront of their minds.

- The natural state of mankind is one of liberty.
- People are born free to do what they want as long as it doesn't impose on the same natural rights of others.

- Governments only exist to protect this natural state of individual freedom.
- Governments have no power other than that voluntarily provided by the citizens who choose to submit to a governing authority.
- Kings and other royals are intrinsically unfair and self-centered, as no one can be born into a position of authority over others.

And so on... As discussed earlier in the book, part of the compromise reached during the constitutional ratification process was establishing a Bill of Rights.

The original Bill of Rights only applied to the Federal government, not state governments. Over the past two centuries, court decisions and subsequent amendments have gradually "incorporated" state government into most of the original Bill of Rights clauses.

Preamble to the Bill of Rights

When reading the Preamble to the Bill of Rights, you can almost detect a "fine, have it your way" undertone. Federalists in support of the Constitution felt the whole idea of natural rights protection was such a "given" that details didn't require enumeration. They believed if you made a list of what was proper or not, then you'd open a bottomless can of worms. If you say freedom of speech is protected, does that imply that freedom of thought or daydreams doesn't exist because those freedoms are not explicitly enumerated? The Anti-Federalists were skeptical and felt certain individual protections, judicial restrictions, and limitations on governmental power should be clearly spelled out.

The result was a compromise. The Constitution was ratified without the Bill of Rights, but there was an expectation that one would be created post haste. And it was. Thus arrived the first ten amendments to the United States Constitution, otherwise known as the Bill of Rights. That ratification process took over two years, finishing on December 15, 1791.

There were 12 amendments submitted for inclusion in the original Bill of Rights, but only ten were ultimately ratified. The first two addressed congressional compensation (shock!) and the number of constituents for Representatives. While some states ratified one or both of these amendments, not enough did for their inclusion in the original Bill of Rights.

1st: Freedoms of Press, Speech, and Religion

Few things are more misunderstood than the First Amendment. What's incredible is that it contains just 45 words, yet arguably it covers more theoretical ground and generates more television pundit arguments than all the others combined. Seriously, can a day go by that you don't hear both jeers and cheers about someone's "right to free speech?"

Alternatively, we frequently talk about the "separation of church and state." Here's a trivia fact. That phrase is nowhere in the Constitution. Let's take a quick detour. That "separation" phrase came from an 1802 letter from Thomas Jefferson to the Danbury Baptists.

> *"I contemplate with sovereign reverence that act of the whole American people which declared that their legislature should 'make no law respecting an establishment of religion, or prohibiting the free exercise thereof,' thus building a wall of separation between Church & State."*

Let's take a quick look at the six topics addressed in the First Amendment.

1. Congress can't make any laws that establish any particular religion. That sounds simple enough, right? If Hollywood celebrities ever overrun Congress, we're all constitutionally protected from any new acts establishing

the Spiritual Actors Guild as the preferred national religion.

2. The government cannot prohibit the free exercise of religion. That prohibition assumes that no one else's natural rights will be infringed upon in the process of practicing religion. Sorry folks, if you choose to follow the Church of Punching Random Strangers in the Nose, your religious practices aren't going to be constitutionally protected.

3. The government cannot place restrictions on your freedom to speak your mind. So, say what you mean to say. Or say it with a Hallmark if that floats your boat. Yeah, I know, you can't yell "fire" in a crowded theater and all that. Don't read too much into this one. You're free to speak your mind, but that doesn't mean you are free from the consequences of your speech. For example, if your job is to answer the phones for Domino's Pizza, you can say whatever you want to irritable customers, but Domino's can also fire you for your speech choices. One could write an encyclopedia set just on this clause, given the plethora of topics that have zipped through the Supreme Court, covering everything from campaign pamphlets to school policies to obscenity to flag burning.

4. The government cannot control the press, no matter how much officials might not like what the press has to say. While, at times during our history, the White House has placed discreet phone calls to major publication editors requesting suppression or delay of reporting, the press is under no government authority. That applies just like the other provisions, with the underlying assumption that the press doesn't infringe on the rights of others while doing their job. To be clear, if the press ticks someone off by their reporting, they're not necessarily infringing on their rights. Remember, rights are high-level, undeniable things, like living.

5. Turn on the news. See any stories about protests and demonstrations? As long as everyone is behaving peaceably and, you guessed it, the activity does not infringe on the natural rights of others, that gathering is constitutionally protected.
6. Everyone has the right to gripe at the government. That's a relief, considering that it's a national pastime. Of course, there's no requirement for the government to act on, or even listen to, the complaints.

While the First Amendment guarantees the right of freedom of speech, it doesn't imply there are never consequences. President William Henry Harrison gave his right to free speech a long workout with a 90-minute inauguration speech—the longest on record. However, after getting sick, possibly from the cold weather that day, he died just one month after assuming office.

2nd: The Right to Own Guns

If there's an amendment that causes more argument than the first, it might be the second. The Second Amendment protects the right to keep and bear arms. People fight over precisely what the second means, but much of the angst stems from the natural evolution of terminology over the years. How we use words, even the same words, changes over the long haul. Consider these examples:

You used to get "sick" with the flu, or maybe a mild case of bunions. Or you might get "sick" of some person or thing, like Piers Morgan or perhaps Madonna. In current terminology, cool things like cars, video games and half-pipe snowboard tricks are "sick." This particular word hasn't just evolved; it's taken on an opposite meaning.

Once upon a name, "dick" was either a proper name or a synonym for "detective." If you called someone "Dick," you wouldn't get punched in the face unless the "dick" caught you robbing a bank.

The point is that commonly accepted meanings of words change over the years.

The same vocabulary confusion applies to the Second Amendment.

Most of the arguments stem from the misunderstanding of two words in this clause: "militia" and "regulated." Back in the day, the term militia referred to the collection of citizens and in no way, shape, or form was descriptive of a government-controlled armed force. In fact, standing armies were not to be trusted—the framers of the Constitution had just fought and died getting out from under the thumb of the world's most powerful standing army. They had no desire to make that mistake again.

As for "well regulated," you might think of that in terms of "properly functioning," like a finely tuned watch. The word "regulated" had nothing to do with governmental control or oversight. Remember, the thinking of the day was precisely the opposite—the government should have little if any, control over much of anything related to the individual. Who do you think provided the cannons used by the Colonial Army? That's right; they were privately owned.

All rights, as described in the Constitution, pertain to individuals only because the government doesn't (and can't) have rights. While today we use "regulated" most frequently to mean "controlled," the word still occasionally serves in its original capacity. Consider Activia yogurt as pitched by Jamie Lee Curtis. It keeps you "well regulated," but we all know government provides no oversight of one's digestion, although it's been known to cause indigestion.

> Having just escaped the heavy hand of the British Army, there was a deep mistrust of a central standing military. According to James Madison's daily notes on the Constitutional Convention proceedings, on August 18, Mr. Luther Martin and Mr. Elbridge Gerry moved that the standing army should not number more than two or three thousand men. We can only assume a bit of sarcasm in General Pinckney's response when he asked whether no troops were ever to be raised until AFTER an attack should be made.

3rd: Housing Soldiers?

This amendment states that the army can't force you to house and feed soldiers. Even though a photo of a couple of grizzled and muddy

Army Rangers sleeping in your Cinderella-themed kid's room might make for the most viral Instagram post ever, it's not going to happen unless you offer military B&B services voluntarily.

The Third Amendment is a bit hard to fathom today as the Marines generally don't requisition our guest rooms when they're in the neighborhood. That's a good thing because few of us could afford to buy enough frozen taquitos to feed a couple of platoons of jarheads on the march. At the time, the colonists were still hacked off about the Quartering Act of 1765, which required them to house and feed British soldiers, hence this inclusion in the Bill of Rights.

Not all politicians leave office fabulously wealthy. Thomas Jefferson died broke while trying to find creative ways to pay his debts. He embarked on an ambitious plan to place some of his commercial properties into a lottery to raise enough funds to save his precious Monticello, but to no avail. That was sold a few years after his death.

4th: You Got a Warrant?

Think how boring cop shows like Law and Order or Dragnet would be if the bad guy never got to say, "You got a warrant?"

Speaking of warrants, this amendment has its roots in a particularly onerous action implemented by the British Parliament in the 1760s. Called writs of assistance, these "warrants" allowed British warrant holders to search and seize at will, pretty much forever. Oh, and they didn't have to pay for damages if they trashed your place in the process. This practice was one of those straws that broke the colonists' back, helping lead to outright revolution.

The Fourth Amendment clarifies that authorities can't search or seize "their persons, houses, papers and effects." Over the years, court rulings have determined that this protection applies to all sorts of things like blood, DNA, electronic communications, and phone conversations. In fact, with few exceptions, an illegal search may have occurred if your privacy is violated because of some government intrusion.

Courts use a simple test to determine whether privacy has been unduly violated.

1. Did you expect privacy at the time? If you're asleep in your home at 3 am, you probably have a reasonable expectation of privacy. If you step away from others to have a quiet phone call, you can reasonably expect some privacy. If you're a congressman who texts naked pictures of himself, you might have an expectation of privacy, but it's probably an unreasonable one.
2. Was your expectation of privacy reasonable in the eyes of others? If you propose to your girlfriend while at the Red Sox game and are expecting a private and romantic moment, you're gonna be in for a rude awakening when you see yourself on the JumboTron. No, others probably wouldn't agree that you had a reasonable expectation of privacy in this situation.

The seizure part of this amendment certainly applies to property. It also applies to people. When you've been restrained from moving freely according to your will, you've been "seized." For example, if you get arrested by the police, you have been seized, although presumably there has been some compelling suspicion of illegal behavior.

The big "but" in the Fourth Amendment is probable cause. Government authorities can search and seize people and things if there is probable cause. Usually, the police have to get a warrant from the relevant judicial authority by proving there is probable cause that some illegal activity has or is happening. Of course, there are situations where search and seizure are allowed without warrants. Suppose Austin Powers sees Dr. Evil driving a dirty bomb into Jackson, Tennessee, to contaminate the national supply of delicious Pringles Sour Cream & Onion chips. In that case, no one will get too agitated over the lack of a warrant before the police search the Evil-mobile.

There's a nifty legal trick that makes the whole Fourth Amendment self-policing. See what I did there? Any evidence obtained by an illegal search or seizure is normally not admissible in court. As tempting as it might be to break into Scottie Evil's lair to find damning evidence, it won't pay if the goal is to try him in court because nothing found there could be used at trial.

> Some of the 11,000 proposed amendments fall into the category of marginally non-traditional. According to the Constitution Center, "In 1893, U.S. House Representative Lucas Miller from Wisconsin proposed renaming the United States to 'the United States of the Earth.' His reasoning was, 'it is possible for the Republic to grow through the admission of new States into the Union until every Nation on Earth has become part of it.' After proposing the amendment, Miller wasn't nominated for a second term in the House."

5th: Pleading the 5th

Like the First Amendment, the Fifth packs several constitutional protections into a short clause. Here's a quick look in the order they're written.

First, before you can go on trial for a major crime, you must be indicted by a grand jury. That's a group of your peers who look at the evidence presented by the prosecution to decide if a trial is warranted. If you've enlisted in the military, this doesn't apply—they have their own procedures for prosecution and trial.

Oh, and if you go to trial for a crime, you can only face the music once, assuming the process completes. If you're acquitted, you can't be charged with the same crime again. There was a movie about this called *Double Jeopardy*. In it, Libby (Ashley Judd) is framed by her husband for the murder of... her husband. She's arrested, tried, convicted, and sent to prison. In jail, she learns about the double jeopardy clause, meaning that she can now actually kill her husband because she's already been convicted for his "death." If you want to know the rest, give it a watch. To be clear, the double jeopardy clause applies whether one is found innocent or guilty.

If you want to learn about Fifth Amendment protection, watch any congressional hearing where a bunch of self-righteous crooks are grilling some other self-righteous crook. Often, the one on the hot seat will "plead the Fifth." That means they decline to answer a question as it might incriminate them. Simply put, you can't be forced to incriminate yourself by being a witness against... yourself.

The Fifth Amendment also guarantees that due process of law will be applied in the process of arrest, trial and punishment. The exact wording of this clause is simple and doesn't contain all the specific details on exactly how due process is to be achieved.

> "...nor be deprived of life, liberty or property, without due process of law...."

Nonetheless, the basic idea is that notice must be given to the party against which action might be taken, they shall have the opportunity to respond, and an impartial decision-maker shall decide the matter.

Last but not least, if the government needs your land to build a road, power line or Congressional Gentleman's Club, they must compensate you justly and fairly for your property. That's the eminent domain clause.

> It took a while for the Supreme Court to sharpen its skills with cases related to the eminent domain clause in the Fifth Amendment. In the 1876 Kohl v. United States case, the government wanted the land to build a custom house and a new post office building. Kohl, the landowner, didn't want to sell. The Supreme Court upheld the government's authority to claim land, with fair compensation, for public use.

6th: The Right to Hire Lawyers

Since we seem to be stuck in a crime and punishment groove, let's talk about rights protected by the Sixth Amendment. In a nutshell, without it, *Boston Legal* would never have become a hit TV series. Fortunately, the founders foresaw the need for legal drama television and outlined the rights of the accused. Here's what the Sixth Amendment covers.

You have a right to a timely (the original text says "speedy") trial.

You have the right to a public trial: no secret courts and no "judges" without accountability. In short, public trials encourage all parties to behave like good little citizens. What happens in court will be all over the nightly news, so people tend to make at least a passing effort to behave.

You have the right to trial by an impartial jury of your peers. This is why so many of us are called for jury duty, but most of us are weeded out via the screening process. Both prosecution and defense counsel get to veto potential jurors they deem "not impartial enough" for their specific case.

You have the right to be tried in the state and district where the alleged crime was committed.

You have the right to be informed, in detail, what the accusations are against you. If your case goes before a grand jury, the prosecutor can't add a bunch of surprise new charges outside the scope of the original indictment.

You have the right to confront your accuser. If someone has a beef against you and levels charges, they can't remain anonymous or text in the allegations from a Bora Bora beach resort. This clause is mostly about hearsay situations where one person hears from another and testifies to what they said.

In case witnesses aren't keen on testifying on your behalf, you have the legal authority to force them to testify.

You have the right to pay an attorney several hundred dollars per hour to assist with your defense. And, as you know from all the cop shows, if you can't afford an attorney, one will be provided for you.

According to James Madison's notes of the Constitutional Convention proceedings, Ben Franklin proposed on Thursday, June 28, that each session should be opened with a prayer. There was some debate on the topic of whether it was appropriate to start the practice now that the convention had already been going on for a month. Still, Madison's notes show the real reason there had been no opening prayer—there was no money to pay a clergyman.

"Mr. Williamson observed that the true cause of the omission could not be mistaken. The Convention had no funds."

7th: Jury Trials

The Seventh Amendment guarantees the right to a jury trial for federal civil cases where the value of the dispute exceeds $20. While the number of jurors has never been specified, Supreme Court rulings have advised a minimum of six jurors who must rule unanimously.

Another clause in the Seventh Amendment prohibits a court from overturning a finding of fact by the jury. While judges are the ultimate authority on questions of legal principles, the jury has the final say over what the facts of any given case indicate. For example, the judge can correct the jury by telling them they are talking about First Degree Times Square Elmo Abuse rather than Second, but that judge can't correct the jury if they determined Elmo threw the first punch.

This amendment was never formally incorporated to the state level, where most civil cases are tried anyway. It hasn't been an issue as states have voluntarily adopted the right to a jury trial.

Today, that $20 limit equates to about $497.87, given inflation. However, there has never been any pressing need to update this monetary limit specified in the Seventh Amendment.

8th: Bail and Punishment

As with most of the other clauses in the Bill of Rights, the drafters left the pesky details for us to figure out at a later date. For example, the Eighth Amendment states that "excessive bail shall not be required," but it goes no further to specify what amount would be considered excessive. The underlying idea was to make sure that bail was fair and reasonable and within reach of those who were not wealthy. The language for fines is similar—nothing "excessive" is allowed, so you can stop stressing about those overdue library books. You're welcome.

Likewise, the Eighth Amendment protects the right not to be subjected to "cruel and unusual punishments." If you end up in prison and are forced to watch reruns of The Real, call your lawyer. Court decisions over the past couple of hundred years have helped to build consistency into the system, so punishments vary with the severity of the crime. The Eighth Amendment has also come into play in cases regarding prison conditions. As a result, the courts have had to decide if only having tater tots on the prison menu once a week is cruel and unusual.

It's a good thing that the office of the president has no eligibility requirement for a college degree. George Washington never attended college, although he did receive a Surveyor's Certificate from the College of William and Mary.

9th: Power to the People!

Ninth amendment? Hey, we can't think of all the ridiculous ways future political creeps will try to exert power over the people, so we're going to write that, even if we haven't named it here, they can't mess with you. In other words, just because protections aren't enumerated in the Bill of Rights, it doesn't imply that you don't have them. Or you might look at it this way. If there's a question about rights, the default decision goes to the people, not the government.

The Ninth Amendment was added as part of the compromise between the Federalists and Anti-Federalists. The Federalists were concerned calling out specific protections would imply that anything not listed would fall under the power of the government. The Anti-Federalists wanted specific protections written for posterity.

Here's a circular logic scenario to twist your brain. Can an amendment to the Constitution be unconstitutional?

The short answer is no. The 18th and 21st Amendments point to a clear example of that. When the 21st Amendment was being considered (ban-

ning the ban on manufacture, importation and sale of alcohol), the 18th Amendment (prohibition) was already part of the Constitution and therefore "constitutional." So, in some weird theoretical sense, the 21st Amendment went against the Constitution.

There was quite a bit of debate during the creation of the Constitution about how the amendment process would work. Some wanted to change the Constitution text in place, while others preferred to add amendment text that would reference the original text to change its meaning or nullify.

There's always an exception, however. Article V states:

"Provided that no Amendment which may be made prior to the Year One thousand eight hundred and eight shall in any Manner affect the first and fourth Clauses in the Ninth Section of the first Article; and that no State, without its Consent, shall be deprived of its equal Suffrage in the Senate."

10th: Power to the States!

While the Ninth Amendment spells out that rights not enumerated fall to the people by default, the Tenth Amendment performs a similar function for the states.

While the founders realized that the federal government needed certain powers to function and protect the integrity of the union, there was plenty of speculation about the power of the government spiraling out of control. You know, like now. To combat this, the Tenth Amendment reminds everyone that the Constitution spells out the federal government's powers. The states are in charge of anything outside the authority expressly granted to the federal government.

Is it constitutional for a former president to run for another office? Sure, there's nothing in the Constitution to prevent that, even if the president served two terms and was "term-limited" out of office. A couple of past presidents have done exactly that by running for and winning House and Senate seats. In these modern days of $500,000 speaking fees for retired presidents, that practice is unlikely as being a former president is a more lucrative career than running a hedge fund.

17

LATER AMENDMENTS

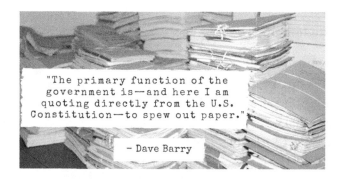

"The primary function of the government is—and here I am quoting directly from the U.S. Constitution—to spew out paper."

– Dave Barry

After the Bill of Rights

The initial ten amendments were passed in bulk and became known as the Bill of Rights. If you were paying close attention, you might take offense at the 10th Amendment being included in the Bill of Rights. Why? It's about states' authority, but states can't have rights; only individuals can have rights. Since it was ratified with the other nine, most people look the other way when including it in the Bill of Rights. It would be awkward to talk about "The Bill of Rights plus that other one."

Starting with the passage of the 11th Amendment, ratified on February 7, 1795, the Constitution has been updated continuously.

The most recent change, the 27th Amendment, came into effect on May 5, 1992. The idea of the 27th wasn't at all new—it took over 202 years for this one to become official.

While only 27 Amendments have been ratified to date, there have been over 11,000 submitted. It's hard for a proposed amendment to make it to the ratification stage since it has to clear one of two complicated hurdles. The first option is that two-thirds of the House and Senate must propose it, and you know they can't even agree on which fork to use first. The other alternative is for two-thirds of states to agree on a proposed amendment at a Constitutional Convention. Only then can a proposed amendment move forward to the ratification stage, where it must be approved by 75% of the states. To date, only 37 amendments have even made it to the beginning of the ratification stage.

11th: State Immunity

The 11th Amendment was a direct response to a power play by the Supreme Court in 1793. It says that the courts don't have authority over a suit brought against a state by an individual in another state. Here's how that went down.

Alexander Chisholm sued the state of Georgia on behalf of the estate of Robert Farquhar. Farquhar had supplied Georgia with gear and supplies during the Revolutionary War, and the estate wanted to get paid. Georgia no-showed because, in their view, they were a sovereign state and couldn't be sued as such.

Sovereign immunity is a concept that prevents countries from suing each other, but in the case of the United States, the underlying assumption behind the Constitution was that each state entered the union voluntarily and as a sovereign entity, much like a country. The Supreme Court ruled on the matter and agreed with Chisholm, citing Article III, Section 2 of the Constitution. If you look at the original text, you'll see the phrase "between a State and Citizens of another State," so, at first glance, it seems that the Supreme Court has jurisdiction over a case like Chisholm v. Georgia because that clause overrode a state's sovereign immunity.

Not so fast, said Congress. They wrote the 11th Amendment not to grant sovereign immunity to states but to reinforce that the states already had it before they volunteered to become part of the union. This amendment was an authoritative smack down on the power of the Supreme Court and was passed on March 4, 1974, and ratified on February 7, 1795.

As with anything involving lawyers that charge by the hour, the devil is in the details. A state can voluntarily agree to a federal trial of this nature. Also, a state's sovereign immunity usually does not extend to cities, towns, counties, school boards and such. Last, issues regarding federal law have been known to circumvent this restriction.

South Carolina was the last state to ratify the 11th Amendment. Could that be because the Chisholm suit originated in South Carolina? Coincidence? We think not.

12th: Voting for Presidents and VPs

The 12th Amendment is about knocking off your political opponents.

OK, that's a slight exaggeration, but it was a legitimate concern. If you remember how the original text of the Constitution spells out the process for electing the president and vice president, you'll recall that electors cast votes for the office of the president only. The vice president's mansion was occupied by the person who came in second place in the presidential election tally.

With that model, it was entirely possible that the top two vote-getters were not friendly and possibly even mortal enemies, at least ideologically. In theory, the system might have created some incentive for the VP to arrange a suspicious accident in order to wear those cool Air Force One jackets. That never happened, but things did get interesting after the 1796 election when Adams, a Federalist, was saddled with Thomas Jefferson, a Democratic-Republican, as his vice president. While there were no reports of poisoned coffee, the two had some vigorous disagreements.

The 1800 election was a mess too, but as the top two were from the same side of the aisle, there was a lengthy tie-breaking process.

The net result of all this was a correction to the system outlined by the 12th Amendment. That specifies electors will cast separate votes for president and vice president. There was one other change. The eligibility requirements for vice president were made identical to those for president. The 12th Amendment was ratified on June 15, 1804.

In the category of "possibly related," there was an effort in 1838 to create a constitutional amendment that banned anyone who had been involved in a duel from holding political office. While political opponents Adams and Jefferson didn't pace off and shoot at each other while serving as president and vice president, the practice was widespread at that time. The proposed anti-dueling amendment didn't gain traction, likely because too many politicians supported the practice. Ah, if only our modern politicians would adopt a more civilized dueling practice today, like water balloon fights or Brazilian Judo on the White House lawn. The Pay Per View revenue alone would wipe out the national debt in weeks.

13th: Slavery Ends

You know what they say about wars, right? The winner gets to write the history books. In a related vein, winners of internal wars are the ones who can change the rules. Known as the Reconstruction Amendments, the 13th, 14th, and 15th addressed the issues of slavery and the still elusive goal of true rights equality.

The 13th Amendment flat-out ended slavery as a legal practice. After the Civil War ended on May 9, 1865, it didn't take long to ratify the 13th Amendment, which Congress had passed on January 31, 1865 —before the official end of the war. Ratification followed shortly after that, on December 6, 1865.

There is an exception written into the brief text. It reads, *"except as punishment for crime whereof the party shall have been duly convicted."* If you're sitting in jail reading this, you'll have to look for another appeal strategy if you were planning on using the 13th to get you out of the slammer.

If you'll remember from Article I, Section 9, Congress put a ticking time bomb into the original Constitution text, making possible an 1808 expiration date on the import of slaves through trade. Clearly, that didn't end the practice, but it started its slow and steady demise.

Ratification was official when Georgia completed the process on December 6, 1865, so the amendment became part of the Constitution, applying to all states in the Union. As ratification only required three-quarters of states, plenty hadn't yet ratified the amendment, although that was largely irrelevant. Interestingly, the final state to ratify the 13th Amendment was Mississippi, finally finishing the paperwork on March 16, 1995. That's right, 1995, not 1895.

14th: Everyone is a Now a Citizen

The second of the Reconstruction Amendments, the 14th, addressed the remaining problems of citizenship and equal treatment under the law for all citizens and other miscellaneous Civil War business. Passed by Congress on June 13, 1866, the 14th Amendment achieved ratification status on July 9, 1868.

The 14th contains four sections, with the first being a real doozy, at least in terms of how many lawsuits rest on it. Suppose you put an infinite number of ambulances in a room with an infinite number of personal injury attorneys. In that case, you'd end up with a similar number of lawsuits as spawned from the first section of the 14th Amendment. We're talking about a broad array of topics such as discrimination, segregation, abortion, same-sex marriage, and even elections.

So, what has that kind of impact on society? Section 1 established four principles:

1. Everyone born or naturalized in the United States is a citizen of both the country and the state in which they live and has the privileges and immunities of full citizens. This included former slaves and their children in the new pool of citizenship.

2. States cannot make any laws that trample on the rights of citizens.
3. States cannot deprive any person of life, liberty, or property without due process of law.
4. Each person in a state's jurisdiction shall have equal protection under the law.

Those look like simple and straightforward concepts, right? Well, there's a lot going on with those simple statements. After the Civil War and ratification of the 13th Amendment that abolished slavery, some bad apples bent the rules by implementing policies designed to suppress the rights of former slaves. They did this using a loophole. Remember, most content in the Constitution and the Bill of Rights only applied to actions of the Federal Government and didn't directly apply to the actions of states. So, some former slave states didn't feel all that motivated to honor the Bill of Rights concepts for all individuals. With us so far?

The 14th Amendment pushed core natural rights protections to the state level. You might have noticed that some text in Section 1 looks familiar to ideas already written in the Constitution and Bill of Rights. That's because, here, it's explicitly targeted at states. Creation and ratification of the 14th Amendment started the long-term process called incorporation, where protections outlined in the Constitution have been pushed down to the state level, so states must adhere to certain behaviors too. No longer can states violate constitutionally protected rights.

Lots of people think that the 14th Amendment is unconstitutional. That sounds like an oxymoron, doesn't it? How can something in the Constitution be unconstitutional? That's kind of like "waking up dead" or saying that "a little pain doesn't hurt."

Part of the reason is that Section 2 of the 14th imposes "representation penalties" on states that disallow males 21 years or older from voting without cause, such as criminal activity or insurrection. That part was intended to make sure that slave states didn't attempt to find ways to prevent newly freed slaves from participating in elections.

Another reason for the unconstitutional Constitution argument stems from some strong-arm tactics used to encourage southern states to toe the new line. Let's just say that some serious pressure was applied to ratify the 14th before former Confederate States players would be readmitted to the halls of Congress. That process gives pause as to whether the methods used to ratify the 14th nullified its status as a legitimate amendment to the Constitution. Then again, there's nothing in the Constitution that says you can't exert political pressure to get things done, provided, of course, that individual rights aren't violated.

Section 2 of the 14th Amendment established new rules about each state's congressional representation. First, that pesky "three-fifths of a person" business got tossed. With the 14th, there was no more counting of slaves as less than a whole person for purposes of representation and taxation. Then again, there were no more slaves, at least not legally.

Second, a gotcha clause discourages former confederate states from suppressing former slaves' right to vote. Suppose a state somehow disrupts the rights of any male (don't worry, ladies, your day comes a few amendments down the road) over 21 years of age from participation in the democratic process. In that case, that state's count for purposes of representation in Washington is diminished by the same number of afflicted voters.

Section 3 reminded participants on the losing side of the Civil War who was now in charge. Any who *"engaged in insurrection or rebellion against the same [United States], or given aid or comfort to the enemies thereof"* were prevented from serving in federal or state government. However, a two-thirds vote by Congress could allow them back in the game. In other words, if you opposed the Union, it's up to Congress whether you could participate in the new world order.

Section 4 cleans up some financial loose ends left over from the war. It specifies any debts incurred by the Union are valid and shall be paid. Debts incurred by the Confederate States of America? Not so much, so if you lent money to that cause, you were out of luck, and no bailouts were likely forthcoming.

Article I, Section 2 of the Constitution and the 14th Amendment reference and exclude "Indians not taxed" when specifying how representatives are allocated to each state. While the phrase isn't clearly defined in the text, it most likely provides a definition of allegiance and authority rather than taxation. Tribes were generally considered to be under their own rule and authority but under the "management and care" (for lack of better words) of the government. Since members weren't under the "authority" of the federal or state governments, then they weren't to be counted for purposes of apportioning Representatives.

15th: Everyone Votes, Period

While the 14th Amendment established penalties for states that prohibited males over 21 from voting, it didn't outright ban the practice. The last of the Reconstruction Amendments, number fifteen, did that.

One of the more straightforward amendments, it says this in its entirety.

> *"The right of citizens of the United States to vote shall not be denied or abridged by the United States or any State on account of race, color, or previous condition of servitude."*

While the 14th Amendment banned direct discrimination based on race, color, or previous servitude status, discrimination practices continued for quite some time. Those not willing to part from the old ways devised all manner of diabolical policies to target minorities, like poll taxes, literacy taxes, and more. While not a direct ban on voting, these practices prevented large segments of minority communities from participating in elections. Future congressional acts and court decisions whittled away at these injustices over the next century.

Note that sex isn't included in the list of voting rights. So far, every reference to voting rights has either outright stated or assumed "males" aged 21 or older. So, as of the 15th Amendment, women still don't have the right to vote. Here's a sneak preview. That problem gets solved four amendments from now.

16th: Taxes, Taxes, and More Taxes

Before ratification of the 16th Amendment, federal taxes were raised at the state level, with each state liable for a share based on its population. If Rhode Island housed two percent of the national population, it would be responsible for two percent of the overall federal tax. With this new change, Congress was unchained from this perceived limitation on their ability to take your money. The 16th Amendment started the ball rolling on what we now deal with today—direct taxation at the whim of our representatives in Washington, D.C.

The 16th Amendment was not ratified until 1913, so taxes were a whole different ball game before that time. Like lice and warts, taxes have been around forever in various forms. Remember that Stamp Taxes and Tea Taxes had a little something to do with the whole American Revolution. While people like to say that federal income tax didn't begin until after the 16th Amendment, that's not true. There were income taxes during the Civil War and again in the 1890s. It's just that many believed these to be unconstitutional. After ratification of the 16th Amendment, the Revenue Act of 1913 kicked off the federal income tax we all know and love today.

17th: Voting for Senators

The 17th Amendment is pretty simple. Initially, when we needed to pick 100 people to leave their daily routines, head to Washington DC, and serve the public by perpetually investigating each other, each state legislature would pick two individuals to serve as senators. Article I, Section 2 of the Constitution outlined this version of the political draft process.

Congress passed the 17th Amendment on May 13, 1912, and it was ratified on April 8, 1913. Apparently, state legislatures were too busy with the important work of naming schools and had little time to choose senators to dispatch to Washington. With the implementation of the 17th, senators were now elected by the people directly. It's the process we know and love to this day, although the 17th Amendment never specified who is responsible for picking up all the leftover campaign signs.

There's one more clause in the 17th Amendment. Suppose there's a mid-term vacancy in the Senate, from death, retirement, resignation, or perhaps a tantalizing finale to one of those never-ending political scandals. In that case, that state's Governor can appoint an interim senator. That person fills the role until an election is scheduled.

> The word *Senator is derived from the Latin word Senatus. Loosely translated, it means "highest council of the state in ancient Rome." However, there's more to the story. Senatus also translates to something along the lines of "council of elders." That word was likely chosen because the Latin word for "of old age" is senilis. So, ipso facto e. Pluribus Unum, the words "senate" and "senile" mean pretty much the same thing. The more you know...*

18th: No More Alcohol

The 18th Amendment elevated the concept of "last call" to a whole new level.

This proposed amendment, passed by Congress in December 1917, banned the manufacture, sale, transportation, import, and export of all "intoxicating liquors" in and from the United States and its territories. While aggressive, this amendment at least provided citizens a grace period to party like there would be no booze tomorrow. See, to make sure the process was familiar to barflies everywhere, a "last call" provision was included. Instead of 30 minutes, this one lasted for a year. The 18th Amendment was ratified by the states on January 16, 1919, thereby launching over a decade of organized crime, secret speakeasies, and plenty of moonshining, not to mention an uptight populace.

The United States fertility rate dropped like a depth charge during Prohibition. In fact, the rate didn't fall lower until those long gas lines of the early 1970s energy crisis. OK, there was the whole Great Depression thing too, but it's far more interesting to assign the blame to a chronic beer shortage.

19th: You've Come a Long Way Baby

Susan B. Anthony, with a good deal of help from her friends and associates, prompted Senator Aaron Sargent from California to introduce what would later become the 19th Amendment.

Yes, the 19th Amendment established that the right to vote should not be denied because of one's sex. When the 19th Amendment was ratified in 1920, 15 states, mainly those in the western territories, already recognized a woman's right to vote. Ratification took care of the rest in one fell swoop.

Before we share these little gems, can we all agree not to shoot the messenger? OK, good. Then here goes...

Before, during, and after the founding years, women's voting rights were essentially non-existent. The underlying rationale for this was the concept of coverture. William Blackstone explained coverture like this:

"By marriage, the husband and wife are one person in the law: that is, the very being or legal existence of the woman is suspended during the marriage, or at least is incorporated and consolidated into that of the husband: under whose wing, protection, and cover, she performs every thing."

Yes, if you read that and see it as code for "we're guys, and we want to continue to remain in charge, but we're going to do that using a thinly veiled scheme of defining marriage as a grand and glorious union between man and woman that makes them one voting entity. Oh, and by the way, the man makes the rules and therefore casts a vote for the team..." you're probably right. Whatever the reason, votes cast by women remained few and far between.

There were exception conditions in some states for various reasons. For example, single women who owned property could sometimes vote. In

other cases, widows were allowed to vote, especially if they independently
owned property. Some of the underlying logic was that "since the husband
was no longer around to guide her, she ought to be able to vote on her
own." Remember, ladies; I asked you nicely not to shoot the messenger.

In some cases, the right to vote was arguably accidental. Ambiguous
language in the state Constitution didn't explicitly limit voting to men
only, so women voted in New Jersey from 1797 to 1807, when the practice
was finally banned by the state legislature.

20th: Lame Duck Sessions

Lame duck sessions are not only unproductive, but they can also be
bad for the country. A lame-duck session is the period that starts after
an election and continues until the newly elected official takes office.
Congress Critters, presidents and VPs who have just been fired by
voters (or sometimes retired due to term limits) still hold office and
associated powers for a couple of months.

In theory, it shouldn't matter because we all know that our elected
officials hold themselves to the highest moral standards and would
never shirk their duties or misbehave during a lame duck phase. In
reality, no one listens to those voted out because they no longer hold
any real influence. In the worst case, some may even cause damage by
supporting unpopular measures that might go against the will of the
people. They've already been "fired" or retired, so what's the difference? They don't have to worry about reelection.

Wanting to minimize the lame duck effect, the 20th Amendment
sets new dates for transitions of the president, vice president, and
members of Congress. Congressional terms end at noon on January
3rd, so newly elected officials take office at 12:01 pm on the same day.
Presidents finish up at noon on January 20th.

Section 2 of the 20th Amendment lays down the law on congressional work days. It specifies that Congress has to convene at least
once per year, starting on January 3 or another day they appoint.
Wow, demanding schedule, eh?

There's still about a two-and-a-half-month period between election day and when a new president is sworn into office. The 20th

Amendment also clarifies what to do should the president-elect die during that time. Section 3 states that the vice president will be sworn in as president. If the president-elect is found to be ineligible, then the vice president-elect is sworn in as acting president.

Sections 3 and 4 also specify Congress has the power to make laws about succession details. You may have seen TV dramas that address the problem of what to do if neither the president nor vice president can perform their duties. And you may have heard that certain individuals are always stowed away in safe off-site locations during major political events like the annual State of the Union Address. If the Capitol building fell into a giant sinkhole during the speech, the "designated survivor" would be available to assume the duties of the presidency. The exact pecking order of the chain of succession is not directly written into the Constitution, although the process for determining that order is.

The Presidential Succession Act of 1947 states the current succession rules, although two prior acts did the same.

Since Washington dwellers always have to argue about something, there is more than a bit of disagreement about whether the current presidential succession list is constitutional. Why? Primarily because congressional officials are the first two on the list! Many constitutional scholars believe they are ineligible for service in the executive branch.

That's because Article II, Section 1 states that only "officers" may serve as a presidential successor. Article I, Section 6 states that elected officials can't be named as "officers" of the United States during their term. Hmmm. Then again, is it really a surprise that Congress created a law to put themselves at the very top of the presidential succession hierarchy? Let's all apply our shocked faces in 3... 2... I...

Ever wondered about the order of presidential succession? Here's the current ranking of designated survivors. If the priority order looks unusual, that's because cabinet positions are ranked in the order in which their respective departments came into being. That's why the Secretary of Homeland Security is last; it's the newest agency.

1. *Speaker of the House of Representatives*
2. *Senate President pro tempore*
3. *Secretary of State*
4. *Secretary of the Treasury*
5. *Secretary of Defense*
6. *Attorney General*
7. *Secretary of the Interior*
8. *Secretary of Agriculture*
9. *Secretary of Commerce*
10. *Secretary of Labor*
11. *Secretary of Health and Human Services*
12. *Secretary of Housing and Urban Development*
13. *Secretary of Transportation*
14. *Secretary of Energy*
15. *Secretary of Education*
16. *Secretary of Veterans Affairs*
17. *Secretary of Homeland Security*

21st: No More "No More Alcohol"

Prohibition? That's old news! The 21st Amendment repealed the 18th Amendment, which, as you might recall, banned the production, transport, and sale of "intoxicating liquors."

For 13 years, not one drop of alcohol was produced or consumed in the entire United States of America. Just kidding. While the drinking rates declined, people still drank like fish. Not only that, a slew of new problems like organized crime related to providing much desired illegal "intoxicating liquors" sprouted up like Whack-a-Moles. Eventually, Congress tired of people like Al Capone getting rich from illegal booze while the politicians lost the ability to tax it. The solution? Make alcohol legal again and stuff the federal coffers with new tax revenue.

Drinking was never illegal during Prohibition. Remember, it was the "manufacture, sale, or transportation of intoxicating liquors" that the 18th Amendment banned. As a result, all sorts of enterprising barkeeps devised ways to dodge the law. For example, "medicinal" alcohol was still legal. Not coincidentally, all sorts of new "diseases" only treatable with alcohol sprouted up.

Oh, and have you ever heard the phrase "booze cruise?" That was another entrepreneurial victory. Customers could take a boat ride to see that invisible line in the sea that marked the edge of international waters. Since there wasn't much to see, the ship would then drive around in circles while passengers drank themselves into oblivion. The best part was that the ship's doctor didn't even have to prescribe Gin & Tonics and Manhattans for seasickness—they were legal at sea.

22nd: Presidential Term Limits

Have you ever noticed how new presidents go into office all fresh and full of vigor? Have you noticed how (especially two-term) presidents leave their posts looking 85 years older? Since eight years in office can age them by 150 years or so, someone thought it might be a good idea to establish limits on how many times they can run for the office of president. There's also the issue of power. The longer a president is in office, the greater the possibility they will want to stay there. You know what they say, power corrupts, and absolute power corrupts baby-kissers absolutely.

Right on the heels of Franklin Delano Roosevelt's whopping 4-0 victory streak (that's four straight presidential election wins), Congress passed the 22nd Amendment. Ratified on February 27, 1951, this one limits a president to two terms. There's a little bit of fine print to cover scenarios where a vice president may assume the office mid-term and such, but the basic idea remains. If you want to get technical about it, a vice president who becomes president with two years or less remaining in the term could possibly hold the office of president for ten years, assuming two election wins. Twice is enough for any sane person, though, isn't it?

If you think too many modern presidents are narcissists, consider this. One of the titles for the job discussed during the Constitutional Convention was "His Highness the President of the United States of America and Protector of their Liberties." Imagine how a title like that would go to people's heads. We're not even sure all that would fit on the Presidential Seal, and that alone might create a constitutional crisis. Can you imagine the size of the campaign buttons? Oh, and how would we paint all that on Air Force One?

23rd: DC Gets To Vote

In 1960, people figured out that many folks live in the District of Political Infighting, also known as the District of Columbia. The 2016 population estimate was somewhere over 681,000. That's more than the entire state of Vermont and significantly more than the state of Wyoming. In case you were wondering, the estimated populations of those two states as of 2016 were 624,000 and 585,000.

Here's the thing. All those government employees pay tax like the rest of us, but until the 23rd Amendment was ratified on March 29, 1961, those folks couldn't vote in presidential elections. With this change, the District of Columbia became entitled to the same number of electors as a state of the equivalent population.

There are a couple of catches, however. No matter how many bureaucrats jam themselves into the city limits, the District can't have more electors than the smallest state. Oh, and they're not considered a state, so they don't get a star on the American flag.

Since what goes on in the District of Columbia seems to correlate so closely with extreme drunkenness, it seems like a good time to share this funny but entirely true bit of constitutional history.

The award for pranking a potential constitutional amendment goes to an unknown author who penned some handwritten additions to an actual proposal from Representative Gomer Smith of Oklahoma.

On April 21, 1938, Representative Smith proposed an amendment to outlaw drunkenness. Section 1 of the article read, "Drunkenness in the United States and all Territories thereof is hereby prohibited." The hand-written notes at the bottom suggest that "the period of time hereby known as Saturday night is hereby stricken from the calendars of the United States" and that Congress shall have the "power to change human nature from time to time." If you're so inclined, you can see a scanned version of the document and its handwritten edits online at catalog.archives.gov.

24th: Everyone Votes, Period, Part II

Remember the 15th Amendment?

> *"The right of citizens of the United States to vote shall not be denied or abridged by the United States or by any State on account of race, color, or previous condition of servitude."*

Some former confederate states devised tricky ways to suppress voting by minorities and the poor. While these states were adhering to the letter of the 15th Amendment, they were continuing to violate its spirit. Poll taxes had been in use for 75% of forever in various forms. Whether one had to own property to vote or show a net worth of 50 pounds (yes, that was real in some states back in the day), the idea was that those who "have" may vote. Those who "have less" may not.

More modern poll taxes didn't require land ownership but implemented fees (taxes) to vote. While the poll tax amount was the same for everyone, it was easier to afford for those in the upper crust of society. Those scraping by often had to choose between eating and voting. Worse yet, some states implemented cumulative poll taxes. If you didn't pay one year, your balance would accrue, and you'd owe twice as much the next election. That pretty much guaranteed the poor had little realistic opportunity to cast a vote never in the history of ever.

The 24th Amendment banished this practice with great clarity, stating that voting rights "shall not be denied or abridged by the United States or any State by reason of failure to pay a poll tax or other tax." The 24th Amendment was ratified in 1964.

Speaking of income...

During the Great Depression, the topic of income equality was often front and center in the political arena. In 1933, Washington Representative

Wesley Lloyd offered a proposed constitutional amendment limiting income to one million dollars. Any money earned above and beyond was to be applied to the national debt.

25th: Presidential Succession

The 25th Amendment was proposed and ratified to make the movie *Air Force One* even more dramatic. OK, maybe not, but the whole question of a "disabled" or "incapacitated" president was a big part of the movie's plot.

But seriously, there were a couple of glaring ambiguities in the backup president's plan. On paper, it sounds easy. The Vice President takes over if things go down the toilet with the first string.

The original constitutional text specifies that the vice president takes over the president's duties, but it wasn't particularly clear whether the vice president actually becomes the new president.

There was also the question of temporary incapacitation. In the movie *Air Force One*, ass-kicking President Harrison Ford is trapped in the cargo hold of his plane, which is now controlled by evil terrorists. Accordingly, it was tough for him to handle the critical paperwork duties of being the president since terrorists had control of all the plane's communications equipment.

The 25th Amendment aimed to resolve some of these uncertainties. Not coincidentally, this became a hot topic shortly after the Kennedy assassination. People started to wonder what would have happened if Kennedy had survived but had been incapacitated. Would he remain in charge? Would the vice president become the president or just assume the duties?

Anyway, the 25th Amendment clearly states right off the bat that in the event a sitting president dies, then the vice president becomes the new president. With that move, there's now a vacancy in the vice presidential mansion, so the amendment specifies that the new president can nominate a replacement vice president. After majority votes confirm that person in the House and Senate, they get to move into the veep cabana.

Here's a great happy hour trivia question sure to stump at least some of your friends, at least the ones who spend more time watching The Daily Show rather than the news.

Who is the only person to serve as vice president and president without ever being elected to either office?

Give up? That would be President Gerald Ford. When Vice President Spiro Agnew resigned in October 1973, President Nixon nominated Ford as the new vice president. When Nixon resigned, Ford became president.

Section 3 creates a clear way to handle temporary incapacitation. The president can transfer power to the vice president with written notice to the president pro tempore of the Senate and the Speaker of the House of Representatives. This gets used frequently in the case of scheduled medical procedures when the president will be under anesthesia for a short period.

Section 4 outlines the procedure for involuntary situations. The vice president, with the majority support of the cabinet, can notify Senate and House leadership that the vice president will assume the presidency. For example, when President Reagan was shot in 1981, that incident would have been a perfect scenario for Section 4 because Reagan, having just been shot and going into surgery, was in no position to be sending letters to Congress arranging a temporary transfer of power. Vice President Bush was in transit, so logistics were a challenge. By the time things settled, Reagan was out of surgery, and the issue was moot. In the movie *Air Force One*, some cabinet members pressured the vice president to assume power, but she resisted, knowing that Harrison Ford always emerges from blockbuster movies victorious.

26th: 18-year-olds Vote

If you're old enough to go to war and pay taxes...

The 26th Amendment was passed by Congress on March 23, 1971, and sailed through the ratification process, achieving adult amendment status on July 1, 1971. Simply put, it says there can be no voting discrimination against anyone 18 or older. States can allow those younger to vote if they want; they just don't have to.

So, as of this writing, as of age 18, you're old enough to be drafted, old enough to pay taxes, and old enough to vote, but not yet old enough to drink beer.

The youngest person to sign the Constitution was Jonathan Dayton representing New Jersey. He was just 26 years old at the time.

27th: Congressional Pay Raises

The 27th Amendment was the original Second Amendment. Remember when we discussed how 12 Amendments were submitted as the original Bill of Rights? The first two weren't ratified, so ten made it through. Since no expiration was specified, this one finally completed the process in 1992, a whopping 203 years after it was submitted to the states for ratification. Who says government moves slower than a senator reaching for the check?

The 27th specifies that if Congress changes its compensation, it can't take effect until after the next election. We're not sure that matters, as most of them remain in office for 75% of forever anyway.

So, let's get this straight. Congress can't vote themselves a pay raise, at least not immediately, yet they still manage to get filthy rich while in office. It's a miracle, isn't it?

Congress hasn't always been a lucrative career. Initially, the idea was to perform those duties part-time while one earned a living doing honest work. The founders' ideas never included the concept of career politicians. In fact, working in Congress was largely a part-time endeavor for nearly 200 years. The early pay scales certainly reflected this idea. From 1789 to 1815, the pay for a United States Senator was just $6 per day.

18

THE CONSTITUTION TODAY

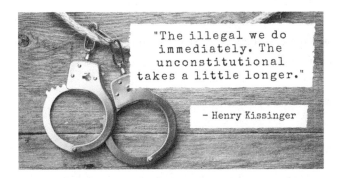

"The illegal we do immediately. The unconstitutional takes a little longer."

– Henry Kissinger

A Constitutional Government?

After reading through the underlying conditions and reasons for the development of the Constitution as we know it, you may have noticed that the government looks and acts a little differently today than what the original rule book might imply.

Given the original intent, one might ask, what would a constitutionally consistent government look like now?

The government would be smaller.

A lot smaller. If the founders knew that the Government would represent 17 percent of our national workforce, we'd likely already be finished with the Second American Revolution.

There would be no career politicians.

We wouldn't be listening to daily news sound bites from career politicians who have been in office for 20 or 30 years. Our first president refused to serve without "term limiting" himself. Thomas Jefferson wrote this.

> "I apprehend that the total abandonment of the principle of rotation in the offices of president and senator will end in abuse. But my confidence is that there will for a long time be virtue and good sense enough in our countrymen to correct abuses."

No, politics was never intended to be a career.

We'd have fewer laws and rules.

We'd have far fewer rules and a lot more accountability. With nothing else better to do, congress continues to pass new laws and government agency employees spend all of their time dreaming up new policies preventing people and entities from doing things. Have you ever known Congress to remove laws from the books in any meaningful way? At what point is the weight of the United States Code going to collapse the earth's crust?

The founders' view was the opposite. There was little proactive restriction, but if you did things that negatively affected other people or property, you were held accountable for your actions.

State government would be where the action is.

State governments would be more robust and involved. From day one, the high-level plan was for the federal government to worry about a couple of big concepts like national security, international relations, trade, and resolving disputes among the states. The state government is where the action was intended to be as far as the intersection with our daily lives.

We'd be more responsible for ourselves and our families.

While certainly related to the idea of fewer rules and more accountability, an underlying assumption in the design of our society was that we'd take care of ourselves and not rely on the government to provide for us or solve our problems. If we want to eat, we work. If we want to retire, we save money. If we want a bigger house or nicer car, we figure out how to move into a higher-paying job. If we want to have children, we assume responsibility for their care.

While the founders discussed at great length the idea of temporary welfare for hardship, they assumed that families and churches would shoulder most of the burden of caring for those of us in need, and the government would step in in a far more limited manner.

You'd be hard pressed to find a massive federal agency.

Federal agencies either wouldn't exist or would have a very narrow scope. If you think about it, nearly every federal and state agency violates the entire underlying concept of separation of powers. They make rules like a legislature. While technically, their policies aren't laws, we must abide by them. They execute those rules just like the executive branch implements and manages laws made by Congress. And they prosecute and adjudicate rule violations on their own. In fact, most federal agencies are no different than federal governments over their own individual fiefdoms.

Sure, Congress has "authorized" the creation and operation of federal agencies, so it's not like they popped out of the pavement of

Pennsylvania Avenue like spring tulips. However, one might argue that when the founders created legislative power in Congress, they didn't intend for us to destroy the concept of separation of powers in the process.

Consider the Transportation Security Administration as a classic example. I'm pretty sure that Congress hasn't made any laws that mandate free gropings each time we choose to travel. Yet, the TSA manages the day-to-day activities of deciding who gets to sweat on a plane while paying exorbitant rates for lousy sandwiches. And the same TSA agents are the ones who decide if we've violated rules.

If you don't believe me, try bringing your breakfast yogurt on your next flight. When your Yoplait is confiscated (because National Security!), try arguing that your forcibly imposed starvation is illegal under the Fourth Amendment. Then ask for a speedy trial by your peers to argue that there's no federal law against eating yogurt while in transit to a different state. You could bring up the Ninth Amendment and argue to the growing audience of enforcement officers that just because the Bill of Rights doesn't expressly say that you have the right to eat yogurt doesn't mean that the federal government has power over your breakfast habits. You get the idea. All that goes out the window when dealing with a federal agency.

That's an admittedly exaggerated example, although you'll most certainly wind up in jail if you refuse to surrender your Yoplait.

There would be lots of other differences; these are just some of the more obvious ones. In summary, we may have experienced just a bit of government bloat over the past couple of centuries.

How much has the government grown since the Constitution went into action? In 1792, total (federal) government spending was $5.1 million. In 2017, gross federal spending was $4.062 trillion. To put that in perspective, that's four million million. Or you might see that as 796,470 times more than spent in 1792.

The population has increased by a factor of about 81, from 4 million to 324 million, but government spending has increased by a factor of 796,470. That's government math for you...

How is the Constitution Relevant Now?

So how is all this constitutional knowledge relevant today? The answer lies in the first sentence of the Declaration of Independence.

> *When in the Course of human events, it becomes necessary for one people to argue about politics incessantly...*

OK, so after reading this book, you know it doesn't say that. However, the Constitution does (really) open with this gem.

> *We the People of the United States, in order to form a more perfect Union, establish Justice, insure domestic Tranquility, provide for the common defence, promote the general Welfare, and secure the Blessings of Liberty to ourselves and our Posterity, do ordain and establish this Constitution for the United States of America.*

And therein lies the answer, stated as the ultimate goal of all the fighting, brainstorming, debate, and contemplation over the Constitution. The whole point is to create a better society that secures the "Blessings of Liberty" for all of us. We've talked at length about what liberty is and is not in this book. Liberty represents an opportunity to do what we choose, provided that we don't infringe on the liberty of others.

The debate between liberty, society, and voluntary forfeiture of rights will probably never end. Perhaps that's one of the reasons that the founders included a way for us to change the Constitution itself. If we, as a society, choose to forfeit additional layers of our natural rights for the benefit of all, then we can make it official by amending the Constitution. Now you know how to do that.

We hope you've enjoyed this simple and (relatively) concise explanation of the founding principles and manual of instructions for the United States of America. Now, when you hear someone talk about something being "constitutional" or "not constitutional," you'll know the real truth.

While our explanations offer a simple but accurate representation, we encourage you to reference the original text of the Declaration of Independence, Constitution, Bill of Rights, and later amendments. Those documents are reproduced in the next chapter for your convenience.

Oh, One More Thing...

I hope you enjoyed the book. While it was an epic amount of work, I had a great time doing it and intend to produce many more like it.

If you enjoyed The Practical Guide to the United States Constitution, I would appreciate you leaving a review with the retailer where you purchased this book. You'd be amazed at how much difference thoughtful reviews from readers like you can make.

19

THE ORIGINAL FOUNDING DOCUMENTS

THE DECLARATION OF INDEPENDENCE

IN CONGRESS, July 4, 1776.

The unanimous Declaration of the thirteen United States of America,

When in the Course of human events, it becomes necessary for one people to dissolve the political bands which have connected them with another, and to assume among the powers of the earth, the separate and equal station to which the Laws of Nature and of Nature's God entitle them, a decent respect to the opinions of mankind requires that they should declare the causes which impel them to the separation.

We hold these truths to be self-evident, that all men are created equal, that they are endowed by their Creator with certain unalienable Rights, that among these are Life, Liberty and the pursuit of Happiness. --That to secure these rights, Governments are instituted among Men, deriving their just powers from the consent of the governed, --That whenever any Form of Government becomes destructive of these ends, it is the Right of the People to alter or to abolish it, and to institute new Government, laying its foundation on such principles and organizing its powers in such form, as to them shall seem most likely to effect their Safety and Happiness. Prudence, indeed, will dictate that Governments long established should not be changed for light and transient causes; and accordingly all experience hath shewn, that mankind are more disposed to suffer, while evils are sufferable, than to right themselves by abolishing the forms to which they are accustomed. But when a long train of abuses and usurpations, pursuing invariably the same Object evinces a design to reduce them under absolute Despotism, it is their right, it is their duty, to throw off such Government, and to provide new Guards for their future security.--Such has been the patient sufferance of these Colonies; and such is now the necessity which constrains them to alter their former Systems of Government. The history of the present King of Great Britain is a history of repeated injuries and usurpations, all having in direct object the establishment of an absolute Tyranny over these States. To prove this, let Facts be submitted to a candid world.

He has refused his Assent to Laws, the most wholesome and necessary for the public good.

He has forbidden his Governors to pass Laws of immediate and pressing importance, unless suspended in their operation till his Assent should be obtained; and when so suspended, he has utterly neglected to attend to them.

He has refused to pass other Laws for the accommodation of large districts of people, unless those people would relinquish the right of Representation in the Legislature, a right inestimable to them and formidable to tyrants only.

He has called together legislative bodies at places unusual, uncomfortable, and distant from the depository of their public Records, for the sole purpose of fatiguing them into compliance with his measures.

He has dissolved Representative Houses repeatedly, for opposing with manly firmness his invasions on the rights of the people.

He has refused for a long time, after such dissolutions, to cause others to be elected; whereby the Legislative powers, incapable of Annihilation, have returned to the People at large for their exercise; the State remaining in the mean time exposed to all the dangers of invasion from without, and convulsions within.

He has endeavoured to prevent the population of these States; for that purpose obstructing the Laws for Naturalization of Foreigners; refusing to pass others to encourage their migrations hither, and raising the conditions of new Appropriations of Lands.

He has obstructed the Administration of Justice, by refusing his Assent to Laws for establishing Judiciary powers.

He has made Judges dependent on his Will alone, for the tenure of their offices, and the amount and payment of their salaries.

He has erected a multitude of New Offices, and sent hither swarms of Officers to harrass our people, and eat out their substance.

He has kept among us, in times of peace, Standing Armies without the Consent of our legislatures.

He has affected to render the Military independent of and superior to the Civil power.

He has combined with others to subject us to a jurisdiction foreign to our constitution, and unacknowledged by our laws; giving his Assent to their Acts of pretended Legislation:

For Quartering large bodies of armed troops among us:

For protecting them, by a mock Trial, from punishment for any Murders which they should commit on the Inhabitants of these States:

For cutting off our Trade with all parts of the world:

For imposing Taxes on us without our Consent:

For depriving us in many cases, of the benefits of Trial by Jury:

For transporting us beyond Seas to be tried for pretended offences

For abolishing the free System of English Laws in a neighbouring Province, establishing therein an Arbitrary government, and enlarging its Boundaries so as to render it at once an example and fit instrument for introducing the same absolute rule into these Colonies:

For taking away our Charters, abolishing our most valuable Laws, and altering fundamentally the Forms of our Governments:

For suspending our own Legislatures, and declaring themselves invested with power to legislate for us in all cases whatsoever.

He has abdicated Government here, by declaring us out of his Protection and waging War against us.

He has plundered our seas, ravaged our Coasts, burnt our towns, and destroyed the lives of our people.

He is at this time transporting large Armies of foreign Mercenaries to

compleat the works of death, desolation and tyranny, already begun with
circumstances of Cruelty & perfidy scarcely paralleled in the most
barbarous ages, and totally unworthy the Head of a civilized nation.

He has constrained our fellow Citizens taken Captive on the high Seas
to bear Arms against their Country, to become the executioners of their
friends and Brethren, or to fall themselves by their Hands.

He has excited domestic insurrections amongst us, and has endeavoured
to bring on the inhabitants of our frontiers, the merciless Indian Savages,
whose known rule of warfare, is an undistinguished destruction of all ages,
sexes and conditions.

In every stage of these Oppressions We have Petitioned for
Redress in the most humble terms: Our repeated Petitions have been
answered only by repeated injury. A Prince whose character is thus
marked by every act which may define a Tyrant, is unfit to be the
ruler of a free people.

Nor have We been wanting in attentions to our British brethren.
We have warned them from time to time of attempts by their legislature to extend an unwarrantable jurisdiction over us. We have
reminded them of the circumstances of our emigration and settle-
ment here. We have appealed to their native justice and magnanimity,
and we have conjured them by the ties of our common kindred to
disavow these usurpations, which, would inevitably interrupt our
connections and correspondence. They too have been deaf to the
voice of justice and of consanguinity. We must, therefore, acquiesce in
the necessity, which denounces our Separation, and hold them, as we
hold the rest of mankind, Enemies in War, in Peace Friends.

We, therefore, the Representatives of the united States of America, in General Congress, Assembled, appealing to the Supreme
Judge of the world for the rectitude of our intentions, do, in the
Name, and by Authority of the good People of these Colonies,
solemnly publish and declare, That these United Colonies are, and of
Right ought to be Free and Independent States; that they are
Absolved from all Allegiance to the British Crown, and that all political connection between them and the State of Great Britain, is and
ought to be totally dissolved; and that as Free and Independent

States, they have full Power to levy War, conclude Peace, contract Alliances, establish Commerce, and to do all other Acts and Things which Independent States may of right do. And for the support of this Declaration, with a firm reliance on the protection of divine Providence, we mutually pledge to each other our Lives, our Fortunes and our sacred Honor.

Georgia
Button Gwinnett
Lyman Hall
George Walton
North Carolina
William Hooper
Joseph Hewes
John Penn
South Carolina
Edward Rutledge
Thomas Heyward, Jr.
Thomas Lynch, Jr.
Arthur Middleton
Massachusetts
John Hancock
Maryland
Samuel Chase
William Paca
Thomas Stone
Charles Carroll of Carrollton
Virginia
George Wythe
Richard Henry Lee
Thomas Jefferson
Benjamin Harrison
Thomas Nelson, Jr.
Francis Lightfoot Lee
Carter Braxton
Pennsylvania

Robert Morris
Benjamin Rush
Benjamin Franklin
John Morton
George Clymer
James Smith
George Taylor
James Wilson
George Ross
Delaware
Caesar Rodney
George Read
Thomas McKean
New York
William Floyd
Philip Livingston
Francis Lewis
Lewis Morris
New Jersey
Richard Stockton
John Witherspoon
Francis Hopkinson
John Hart
Abraham Clark
New Hampshire
Josiah Bartlett
William Whipple
Massachusetts
Samuel Adams
John Adams
Robert Treat Paine
Elbridge Gerry
Rhode Island
Stephen Hopkins
William Ellery
Connecticut

Roger Sherman
Samuel Huntington
William Williams
Oliver Wolcott
New Hampshire
Matthew Thornton

THE CONSTITUTION

We the People of the United States, in Order to form a more perfect Union, establish Justice, insure domestic Tranquility, provide for the common defence, promote the general Welfare, and secure the Blessings of Liberty to ourselves and our Posterity, do ordain and establish this Constitution for the United States of America.

Article I

Section 1.

All legislative Powers herein granted shall be vested in a Congress of the United States, which shall consist of a Senate and House of Representatives.

Section 2.

The House of Representatives shall be composed of Members chosen every second Year by the People of the several States, and the Electors in each State shall have the Qualifications requisite for Electors of the most numerous Branch of the State Legislature.

No Person shall be a representative who shall not have attained to the Age of twenty five Years, and been seven Years a Citizen of the United States, and who shall not, when elected, be an Inhabitant of that State in which he shall be chosen.

Representatives and direct Taxes shall be apportioned among the several States which may be included within this Union, according to their respective Numbers, which shall be determined by adding to the whole Number of free Persons, including those bound to Service for a Term of Years, and excluding Indians not taxed, three fifths of all other Persons. The actual Enumeration shall be made within three Years after the first Meeting of the Congress of the United States, and within every subsequent Term of ten Years, in such Manner as they shall by Law direct. The Number of representatives shall not exceed one for every thirty Thousand, but each State shall have at Least one representative; and until such enumeration shall be made, the State of New Hampshire shall be entitled to chuse three, Massachusetts eight, Rhode-Island and Providence Plantations one, Connecticut five, New-York six, New Jersey four, Pennsylvania eight, Delaware one, Maryland six, Virginia ten, North Carolina five, South Carolina five, and Georgia three.

When vacancies happen in the Representation from any State, the Executive Authority thereof shall issue Writs of Election to fill such Vacancies.

The House of Representatives shall chuse their Speaker and other Officers; and shall have the sole Power of Impeachment.

Section 3.

The Senate of the United States shall be composed of two senators from each State, chosen by the Legislature thereof for six Years; and each senator shall have one Vote.

Immediately after they shall be assembled in Consequence of the first Election, they shall be divided as equally as may be into three Classes. The Seats of the senators of the first Class shall be vacated at the Expiration of the second Year, of the second Class at the Expiration of the fourth Year, and of the third Class at the Expiration of the sixth Year, so that one third may be chosen every second Year; and if Vacancies happen by Resignation, or otherwise, during the Recess of the Legislature of any State, the Executive thereof may make temporary Appointments until the next Meeting of the Legislature, which shall then fill such Vacancies.

No Person shall be a senator who shall not have attained to the

Age of thirty Years, and been nine Years a Citizen of the United States, and who shall not, when elected, be an Inhabitant of that State for which he shall be chosen.

The Vice President of the United States shall be President of the Senate, but shall have no Vote, unless they be equally divided.

The Senate shall chuse their other Officers, and also a President pro tempore, in the Absence of the Vice President, or when he shall exercise the Office of President of the United States.

The Senate shall have the sole Power to try all Impeachments. When sitting for that Purpose, they shall be on Oath or Affirmation. When the President of the United States is tried, the Chief Justice shall preside: And no Person shall be convicted without the Concurrence of two thirds of the Members present.

Judgment in Cases of Impeachment shall not extend further than to removal from Office, and disqualification to hold and enjoy any Office of honor, Trust or Profit under the United States: but the Party convicted shall nevertheless be liable and subject to Indictment, Trial, Judgment and Punishment, according to Law.

Section 4.

The Times, Places and Manner of holding Elections for senators and representatives, shall be prescribed in each State by the Legislature thereof; but the Congress may at any time by Law make or alter such Regulations, except as to the Places of chusing senators.

The Congress shall assemble at least once in every Year, and such Meeting shall be on the first Monday in December, unless they shall by Law appoint a different Day.

Section 5.

Each House shall be the Judge of the Elections, Returns and Qualifications of its own Members, and a Majority of each shall constitute a Quorum to do Business; but a smaller Number may adjourn from day to day, and may be authorized to compel the Attendance of absent Members, in such Manner, and under such Penalties as each House may provide.

Each House may determine the Rules of its Proceedings, punish its Members for disorderly Behaviour, and, with the Concurrence of two thirds, expel a Member.

Each House shall keep a Journal of its Proceedings, and from time to time publish the same, excepting such Parts as may in their Judgment require Secrecy; and the Yeas and Nays of the Members of either House on any question shall, at the Desire of one fifth of those Present, be entered on the Journal.

Neither House, during the Session of Congress, shall, without the Consent of the other, adjourn for more than three days, nor to any other Place than that in which the two Houses shall be sitting.

Section 6.

The senators and representatives shall receive a Compensation for their Services, to be ascertained by Law, and paid out of the Treasury of the United States. They shall in all Cases, except Treason, Felony and Breach of the Peace, be privileged from Arrest during their Attendance at the Session of their respective Houses, and in going to and returning from the same; and for any Speech or Debate in either House, they shall not be questioned in any other Place.

No senator or representative shall, during the Time for which he was elected, be appointed to any civil Office under the Authority of the United States, which shall have been created, or the Emoluments whereof shall have been encreased during such time; and no Person holding any Office under the United States, shall be a Member of either House during his Continuance in Office.

Section 7.

All Bills for raising Revenue shall originate in the House of Representatives; but the Senate may propose or concur with Amendments as on other Bills.

Every Bill which shall have passed the House of Representatives and the Senate, shall, before it become a Law, be presented to the President of the United States: If he approve he shall sign it, but if not he shall return it, with his Objections to that House in which it shall have originated, who shall enter the Objections at large on their Journal, and proceed to reconsider it. If after such Reconsideration two thirds of that House shall agree to pass the Bill, it shall be sent, together with the Objections, to the other House, by which it shall likewise be reconsidered, and if approved by two thirds of that House, it shall become a Law. But in all such Cases the Votes of both Houses shall be determined by yeas and Nays, and the Names of the Persons voting for and against the Bill shall be entered on the Journal of each House respectively. If any Bill shall not be returned by the President within ten Days (Sundays excepted) after it shall have been presented to him, the Same shall be a Law, in like Manner as if he had signed it, unless the Congress by their Adjournment prevent its Return, in which Case it shall not be a Law.

Every Order, Resolution, or Vote to which the Concurrence of the Senate and House of Representatives may be necessary (except on a question of Adjournment) shall be presented to the President of the United States; and before the Same shall take Effect, shall be approved by him, or being disapproved by him, shall be repassed by two thirds of the Senate and House of Representatives, according to the Rules and Limitations prescribed in the Case of a Bill.

Section 8.

The Congress shall have Power To lay and collect Taxes, Duties, Imposts and Excises, to pay the Debts and provide for the common Defence and general Welfare of the United States; but all Duties, Imposts and Excises shall be uniform throughout the United States;

To borrow Money on the credit of the United States;

To regulate Commerce with foreign Nations, and among the several States, and with the Indian Tribes;

To establish an uniform Rule of Naturalization, and uniform Laws on the subject of Bankruptcies throughout the United States;

To coin Money, regulate the Value thereof, and of foreign Coin, and fix the Standard of Weights and Measures;

To provide for the Punishment of counterfeiting the Securities and current Coin of the United States;

To establish Post Offices and post Roads;

To promote the Progress of Science and useful Arts, by securing for limited Times to Authors and Inventors the exclusive Right to their respective Writings and Discoveries;

To constitute Tribunals inferior to the supreme Court;

To define and punish Piracies and Felonies committed on the high Seas, and Offences against the Law of Nations;

To declare War, grant Letters of Marque and Reprisal, and make Rules concerning Captures on Land and Water;

To raise and support Armies, but no Appropriation of Money to that Use shall be for a longer Term than two Years;

To provide and maintain a Navy;

To make Rules for the Government and Regulation of the land and naval Forces;

To provide for calling forth the Militia to execute the Laws of the Union, suppress Insurrections and repel Invasions;

To provide for organizing, arming, and disciplining, the Militia, and for governing such Part of them as may be employed in the Service of the United States, reserving to the States respectively, the Appointment of the Officers, and the Authority of training the Militia according to the discipline prescribed by Congress;

To exercise exclusive Legislation in all Cases whatsoever, over such District (not exceeding ten Miles square) as may, by Cession of particular States, and the Acceptance of Congress, become the Seat of the Government of the United States, and to exercise like Authority over all Places purchased by the Consent of the Legislature of the State in which the Same shall be, for the Erection of Forts, Magazines, Arsenals, dock-Yards, and other needful Buildings;--And

To make all Laws which shall be necessary and proper for carrying into Execution the foregoing Powers, and all other Powers vested by this Constitution in the Government of the United States, or in any Department or Officer thereof.

Section 9.

The Migration or Importation of such Persons as any of the States now existing shall think proper to admit, shall not be prohibited by the Congress prior to the Year one thousand eight hundred and eight, but a Tax or duty may be imposed on such Importation, not exceeding ten dollars for each Person.

The Privilege of the Writ of Habeas Corpus shall not be suspended, unless when in Cases of Rebellion or Invasion the public Safety may require it.

No Bill of Attainder or ex post facto Law shall be passed.

No Capitation, or other direct, Tax shall be laid, unless in Proportion to the Census or enumeration herein before directed to be taken.

No Tax or Duty shall be laid on Articles exported from any State.

No Preference shall be given by any Regulation of Commerce or Revenue to the Ports of one State over those of another; nor shall Vessels bound to, or from, one State, be obliged to enter, clear, or pay Duties in another.

No Money shall be drawn from the Treasury, but in Consequence of Appropriations made by Law; and a regular Statement and Account of the Receipts and Expenditures of all public Money shall be published from time to time.

No Title of Nobility shall be granted by the United States: And no Person holding any Office of Profit or Trust under them, shall, without the Consent of the Congress, accept of any present, Emolument, Office, or Title, of any kind whatever, from any King, Prince, or foreign State.

Section 10.

No State shall enter into any Treaty, Alliance, or Confederation; grant Letters of Marque and Reprisal; coin Money; emit Bills of Credit; make any Thing but gold and silver Coin a Tender in Payment of Debts; pass any Bill of Attainder, ex post facto Law, or Law impairing the Obligation of Contracts, or grant any Title of Nobility.

No State shall, without the Consent of the Congress, lay any Imposts or Duties on Imports or Exports, except what may be absolutely necessary for executing it's inspection Laws: and the net Produce of all Duties and Imposts, laid by any State on Imports or Exports, shall be for the Use of the Treasury of the United States; and all such Laws shall be subject to the Revision and Controul of the Congress.

No State shall, without the Consent of Congress, lay any Duty of Tonnage, keep Troops, or Ships of War in time of Peace, enter into any Agreement or Compact with another State, or with a foreign Power, or engage in War, unless actually invaded, or in such imminent Danger as will not admit of delay.

Article II

Section I.

The executive Power shall be vested in a President of the United States of America. He shall hold his Office during the Term of four Years, and, together with the Vice President, chosen for the same Term, be elected, as follows:

Each State shall appoint, in such Manner as the Legislature thereof may direct, a Number of Electors, equal to the whole Number of senators and representatives to which the State may be entitled in the Congress: but no senator or representative, or Person holding an Office of Trust or Profit under the United States, shall be appointed an Elector.

The Electors shall meet in their respective States, and vote by Ballot for two Persons, of whom one at least shall not be an Inhabitant of the same State with themselves. And they shall make a List of all the Persons voted for, and of the Number of Votes for each; which List they shall sign and certify, and transmit sealed to the Seat of the Government of the United States, directed to the President of the Senate. The President of the Senate shall, in the Presence of the Senate and House of Representatives, open all the Certificates, and the Votes shall then be counted. The Person having the greatest Number of Votes shall be the President, if such Number be a Majority of the whole Number of Electors appointed; and if there be more than one who have such Majority, and have an equal Number of Votes, then the House of Representatives shall immediately chuse by Ballot one of them for President; and if no Person have a Majority, then from the five highest on the List the said House shall in like Manner chuse the President. But in chusing the President, the Votes shall be taken by States, the Representation from each State having one Vote; A quorum for this purpose shall consist of a Member or Members from two thirds of the States, and a Majority of all the States shall be necessary to a Choice. In every Case, after the Choice of the President, the Person having the greatest Number of Votes of the Electors shall be the Vice President. But if there should remain two or more who have equal Votes, the Senate shall chuse from them by Ballot the Vice President.

The Congress may determine the Time of chusing the Electors, and the Day on which they shall give their Votes; which Day shall be the same throughout the United States.

No Person except a natural born Citizen, or a Citizen of the United States, at the time of the Adoption of this Constitution, shall be eligible to the Office of President; neither shall any Person be eligible to that Office who shall not have attained to the Age of thirty five Years, and been fourteen Years a Resident within the United States.

In Case of the Removal of the President from Office, or of his Death, Resignation, or Inability to discharge the Powers and Duties of the said Office, the Same shall devolve on the Vice President, and the Congress may by Law provide for the Case of Removal, Death, Resignation or Inability, both of the President and Vice President, declaring what Officer shall then act as President, and such Officer shall act accordingly, until the Disability be removed, or a President shall be elected.

The President shall, at stated Times, receive for his Services, a Compensation, which shall neither be increased nor diminished during the Period for which he shall have been elected, and he shall not receive within that Period any other Emolument from the United States, or any of them.

Before he enter on the Execution of his Office, he shall take the following Oath or Affirmation:—"I do solemnly swear (or affirm) that I will faithfully execute the Office of President of the United States, and will to the best of my Ability, preserve, protect and defend the Constitution of the United States."

Section 2.

The President shall be Commander in Chief of the Army and Navy of the United States, and of the Militia of the several States, when called into the actual Service of the United States; he may require the Opinion, in writing, of the principal Officer in each of the executive Departments, upon any Subject relating to the Duties of their respective Offices, and he shall have Power to grant Reprieves and Pardons for Offences against the United States, except in Cases of Impeachment.

He shall have Power, by and with the Advice and Consent of the Senate, to make Treaties, provided two thirds of the senators present concur; and he shall nominate, and by and with the Advice and Consent of the Senate, shall appoint Ambassadors, other public Ministers and Consuls, Judges of the supreme Court, and all other Officers of the United States, whose Appointments are not herein otherwise provided for, and which shall be established by Law: but the Congress may by Law vest the Appointment of such inferior Officers, as they think proper, in the President alone, in the Courts of Law, or in the Heads of Departments.

The President shall have Power to fill up all Vacancies that may happen during the Recess of the Senate, by granting Commissions which shall expire at the End of their next Session.

Section 3.

He shall from time to time give to the Congress Information of the State of the Union, and recommend to their Consideration such Measures as he shall judge necessary and expedient; he may, on extraordinary Occasions, convene both Houses, or either of them, and in Case of Disagreement between them, with Respect to the Time of Adjournment, he may adjourn them to such Time as he shall think proper; he shall receive Ambassadors and other public Ministers; he shall take Care that the Laws be faithfully executed, and shall Commission all the Officers of the United States.

Section 4.

The President, Vice President and all civil Officers of the United States, shall be removed from Office on Impeachment for, and Conviction of, Treason, Bribery, or other high Crimes and Misdemeanors.

Article III

Section 1.

The judicial Power of the United States shall be vested in one supreme Court, and in such inferior Courts as the Congress may from time to time ordain and establish. The Judges, both of the supreme and inferior Courts, shall hold their Offices during good Behaviour, and shall, at stated Times, receive for their Services a Compensation, which shall not be diminished during their Continuance in Office.

Section 2.

The judicial Power shall extend to all Cases, in Law and Equity, arising under this Constitution, the Laws of the United States, and Treaties made, or which shall be made, under their Authority;--to all Cases affecting Ambassadors, other public Ministers and Consuls;-- to all Cases of admiralty and maritime Jurisdiction;--to Controversies to which the United States shall be a Party;--to Controversies between two or more States;-- between a State and Citizens of another State,-- between Citizens of different States,--between Citizens of the same State claiming Lands under Grants of different States, and between a State, or the Citizens thereof, and foreign States, Citizens or Subjects.

In all Cases affecting Ambassadors, other public Ministers and Consuls, and those in which a State shall be Party, the supreme Court shall have original Jurisdiction. In all the other Cases before mentioned, the supreme Court shall have appellate Jurisdiction, both as to Law and Fact, with such Exceptions, and under such Regulations as the Congress shall make.

The Trial of all Crimes, except in Cases of Impeachment, shall be by Jury; and such Trial shall be held in the State where the said Crimes shall have been committed; but when not committed within any State, the Trial shall be at such Place or Places as the Congress may by Law have directed.

Section 3.

Treason against the United States, shall consist only in levying War against them, or in adhering to their Enemies, giving them Aid and Comfort. No Person shall be convicted of Treason unless on the Testimony of two Witnesses to the same overt Act, or on Confession in open Court.

The Congress shall have Power to declare the Punishment of Treason, but no Attainder of Treason shall work Corruption of Blood, or Forfeiture except during the Life of the Person attainted.

Article IV

Section 1.

Full Faith and Credit shall be given in each State to the public Acts, Records, and judicial Proceedings of every other State. And the Congress may by general Laws prescribe the Manner in which such Acts, Records and Proceedings shall be proved, and the Effect thereof.

Section 2.

The Citizens of each State shall be entitled to all Privileges and Immunities of Citizens in the several States.

A Person charged in any State with Treason, Felony, or other Crime, who shall flee from Justice, and be found in another State, shall on Demand of the executive Authority of the State from which he fled, be delivered up, to be removed to the State having Jurisdiction of the Crime.

No Person held to Service or Labour in one State, under the Laws thereof, escaping into another, shall, in Consequence of any Law or Regulation therein, be discharged from such Service or Labour, but shall be delivered up on Claim of the Party to whom such Service or Labour may be due.

Section 3.

New States may be admitted by the Congress into this Union; but no new State shall be formed or erected within the Jurisdiction of any other State; nor any State be formed by the Junction of two or more States, or Parts of States, without the Consent of the Legislatures of the States concerned as well as of the Congress.

The Congress shall have Power to dispose of and make all needful Rules and Regulations respecting the Territory or other Property belonging to the United States; and nothing in this Constitution shall be so construed as to Prejudice any Claims of the United States, or of any particular State.

Section 4.

The United States shall guarantee to every State in this Union a Republican Form of Government, and shall protect each of them against Invasion; and on Application of the Legislature, or of the

Executive (when the Legislature cannot be convened), against domestic Violence.

Article V

The Congress, whenever two thirds of both Houses shall deem it necessary, shall propose Amendments to this Constitution, or, on the Application of the Legislatures of two thirds of the several States, shall call a Convention for proposing Amendments, which, in either Case, shall be valid to all Intents and Purposes, as Part of this Constitution, when ratified by the Legislatures of three fourths of the several States, or by Conventions in three fourths thereof, as the one or the other Mode of Ratification may be proposed by the Congress; Provided that no Amendment which may be made prior to the Year One thousand eight hundred and eight shall in any Manner affect the first and fourth Clauses in the Ninth Section of the first Article; and that no State, without its Consent, shall be deprived of its equal Suffrage in the Senate.

Article VI

All Debts contracted and Engagements entered into, before the Adoption of this Constitution, shall be as valid against the United States under this Constitution, as under the Confederation.

This Constitution, and the Laws of the United States which shall be made in Pursuance thereof; and all Treaties made, or which shall be made, under the Authority of the United States, shall be the supreme Law of the Land; and the Judges in every State shall be bound thereby, any Thing in the Constitution or Laws of any State to the Contrary notwithstanding.

The senators and representatives before mentioned, and the Members of the several State Legislatures, and all executive and judicial Officers, both of the United States and of the several States, shall be bound by Oath or Affirmation, to support this Constitution; but no religious Test shall ever be required as a Qualification to any Office or public Trust under the United States.

Article VII

The Ratification of the Conventions of nine States, shall be sufficient for the Establishment of this Constitution between the States so ratifying the Same.

Signatures

Attest William Jackson Secretary

Done in Convention by the Unanimous Consent of the States present the Seventeenth Day of September in the Year of our Lord one thousand seven hundred and Eighty seven and of the Independence of the United States of America the Twelfth In witness whereof We have hereunto subscribed our Names,

G. Washington
President and deputy from Virginia

Delaware
Geo: Read
Gunning Bedford jun
John Dickinson
Richard Bassett
Jaco: Broom

Maryland
James McHenry
Dan of St Thos. Jenifer
Danl. Carroll

Virginia
John Blair
James Madison Jr.

North Carolina
Wm. Blount
Richd. Dobbs Spaight
Hu Williamson

South Carolina
J. Rutledge
Charles Cotesworth Pinckney

Charles Pinckney

Pierce Butler

Georgia

William Few

Abr Baldwin

New Hampshire

John Langdon

Nicholas Gilman

Massachusetts

Nathaniel Gorham

Rufus King

Connecticut

Wm. Saml. Johnson

Roger Sherman

New York

Alexander Hamilton

New Jersey

Wil: Livingston

David Brearley

Wm. Paterson

Jona: Dayton

Pennsylvania

B. Franklin

Thomas Mifflin

Robt. Morris

Geo. Clymer

Thos. FitzSimons

Jared Ingersoll

James Wilson

Gouv Morris

THE BILL OF RIGHTS

The Preamble to The Bill of Rights

Congress of the United States

begun and held at the City of New-York, on

Wednesday the fourth of March, one thousand seven hundred and eighty nine.

THE Conventions of a number of the States, having at the time of their adopting the Constitution, expressed a desire, in order to prevent misconstruction or abuse of its powers, that further declaratory and restrictive clauses should be added: And as extending the ground of public confidence in the Government, will best ensure the beneficent ends of its institution.

RESOLVED by the Senate and House of Representatives of the United States of America, in Congress assembled, two thirds of both Houses concurring, that the following Articles be proposed to the Legislatures of the several States, as amendments to the Constitution of the United States, all, or any of which Articles, when ratified by three fourths of the said Legislatures, to be valid to all intents and purposes, as part of the said Constitution; viz.

ARTICLES in addition to, and Amendment of the Constitution of the United States of America, proposed by Congress, and ratified by the Legislatures of the several States, pursuant to the fifth Article of the original Constitution.

Amendment I

Congress shall make no law respecting an establishment of religion, or prohibiting the free exercise thereof; or abridging the freedom of speech, or of the press; or the right of the people peaceably to assemble, and to petition the Government for a redress of grievances.

Amendment II

A well regulated Militia, being necessary to the security of a free State, the right of the people to keep and bear Arms, shall not be infringed.

Amendment III

No Soldier shall, in time of peace be quartered in any house, without the consent of the Owner, nor in time of war, but in a manner to be prescribed by law.

Amendment IV

The right of the people to be secure in their persons, houses, papers, and effects, against unreasonable searches and seizures, shall not be violated, and no Warrants shall issue, but upon probable cause, supported by Oath or affirmation, and particularly describing the place to be searched, and the persons or things to be seized.

Amendment V

No person shall be held to answer for a capital, or otherwise infamous crime, unless on a presentment or indictment of a Grand Jury, except in cases arising in the land or naval forces, or in the Militia, when in actual service in time of War or public danger; nor shall any person be subject for the same offence to be twice put in jeopardy of life or limb; nor shall be compelled in any criminal case to be a witness against himself, nor be deprived of life, liberty, or property, without due process of law; nor shall private property be taken for public use, without just compensation.

Amendment VI

In all criminal prosecutions, the accused shall enjoy the right to a speedy and public trial, by an impartial jury of the State and district wherein the crime shall have been committed, which district shall have been previously ascertained by law, and to be informed of the nature and cause of the accusation; to be confronted with the witnesses against him; to have compulsory process for obtaining witnesses in his favor, and to have the Assistance of Counsel for his defence.

Amendment VII

In Suits at common law, where the value in controversy shall exceed twenty dollars, the right of trial by jury shall be preserved, and no fact tried by a jury, shall be otherwise re-examined in any Court of the United States, than according to the rules of the common law.

Amendment VIII

Excessive bail shall not be required, nor excessive fines imposed, nor cruel and unusual punishments inflicted.

Amendment IX

The enumeration in the Constitution, of certain rights, shall not be construed to deny or disparage others retained by the people.

Amendment X

The powers not delegated to the United States by the Constitution, nor prohibited by it to the States, are reserved to the States respectively, or to the people.

AMENDMENTS 11 - 27

Amendment XI

The Judicial power of the United States shall not be construed to extend to any suit in law or equity, commenced or prosecuted against one of the United States by Citizens of another State, or by Citizens or Subjects of any Foreign State.

Amendment XII

The Electors shall meet in their respective states and vote by ballot for President and Vice President, one of whom, at least, shall not be an inhabitant of the same state with themselves; they shall name in their ballots the person voted for as President, and in distinct ballots the person voted for as Vice President, and they shall make distinct lists of all persons voted for as President, and of all persons voted for as Vice President, and of the number of votes for each, which lists they shall sign and certify, and transmit sealed to the seat of the government of the United States, directed to the President of the Senate; -- the President of the Senate shall, in the presence of the Senate and House of Representatives, open all the certificates and the votes shall then be counted; -- The person having the greatest number of votes for President, shall be the President, if such number be a majority of the whole number of Electors appointed; and if no person have such majority, then from the persons having the highest numbers not exceeding three on the list of those voted for as President, the House of Representatives shall choose immediately, by ballot, the President. But in choosing the President, the votes shall be taken by states, the representation from each state having one vote; a quorum for this purpose shall consist of a member or members from two-thirds of the states, and a majority of all the states shall be necessary to a choice. [And if the House of Representatives shall not choose a President whenever the right of choice shall devolve upon them, before the fourth day of March next following, then the Vice President shall act as President, as in case of the death or other constitutional disability of the President. --] The person having the greatest number of votes as Vice President, shall be the Vice President, if such number be a majority of the whole number of Electors appointed, and if no person have a majority, then from the two highest numbers on the list, the Senate shall choose the Vice President; a quorum for the purpose shall consist of two-thirds of the whole number of Senators, and a majority of the whole number shall be necessary to a choice. But no person constitutionally ineligible to the office of President shall be eligible to that of Vice President of the United States.

Amendment XIII

Section 1.

Neither slavery nor involuntary servitude, except as a punishment for crime whereof the party shall have been duly convicted, shall exist within the United States, or any place subject to their jurisdiction.

Section 2.

Congress shall have power to enforce this article by appropriate legislation.

Amendment XIV

Section 1.

All persons born or naturalized in the United States, and subject to the jurisdiction thereof, are citizens of the United States and of the State wherein they reside. No State shall make or enforce any law which shall abridge the privileges or immunities of citizens of the United States; nor shall any State deprive any person of life, liberty, or property, without due process of law; nor deny to any person within its jurisdiction the equal protection of the laws.

Section 2.

Representatives shall be apportioned among the several States according to their respective numbers, counting the whole number of persons in each State, excluding Indians not taxed. But when the right to vote at any election for the choice of electors for President and Vice President of the United States, Representatives in Congress, the Executive and Judicial officers of a State, or the members of the Legislature thereof, is denied to any of the male inhabitants of such State, being twenty-one years of age,* and citizens of the United States, or in any way abridged, except for participation in rebellion, or other crime, the basis of representation therein shall be reduced in the proportion which the number of such male citizens shall bear to the whole number of male citizens twenty-one years of age in such State.

Section 3.

No person shall be a Senator or Representative in Congress, or elector of President and Vice President, or hold any office, civil or military, under the United States, or under any State, who, having previously taken an oath, as a member of Congress, or as an officer of the United States, or as a member of any State legislature, or as an executive or judicial officer of any State, to support the Constitution of the United States, shall have engaged in insurrection or rebellion against the same, or given aid or comfort to the enemies thereof. But Congress may, by a vote of two-thirds of each House, remove such disability.

Section 4.

The validity of the public debt of the United States, authorized by law, including debts incurred for payment of pensions and bounties for services in suppressing insurrection or rebellion, shall not be questioned. But neither the United States nor any State shall assume or pay any debt or obligation incurred in aid of insurrection or rebellion against the United States, or any claim for the loss or emancipation of any slave; but all such debts, obligations and claims shall be held illegal and void.

Section 5.

The Congress shall have the power to enforce, by appropriate legislation, the provisions of this article.

Amendment XV

Section 1.

The right of citizens of the United States to vote shall not be denied or abridged by the United States or by any State on account of race, color, or previous condition of servitude--

Section 2.

The Congress shall have the power to enforce this article by appropriate legislation.

Amendment XVI

The Congress shall have power to lay and collect taxes on incomes, from whatever source derived, without apportionment among the several States, and without regard to any census or enumeration.

Amendment XVII

The Senate of the United States shall be composed of two Senators from each State, elected by the people thereof, for six years; and each Senator shall have one vote. The electors in each State shall have the qualifications requisite for electors of the most numerous branch of the State legislatures.

When vacancies happen in the representation of any State in the

Senate, the executive authority of such State shall issue writs of election to fill such vacancies: Provided, That the legislature of any State may empower the executive thereof to make temporary appointments until the people fill the vacancies by election as the legislature may direct.

This amendment shall not be so construed as to affect the election or term of any Senator chosen before it becomes valid as part of the Constitution.

Amendment XVIII

Section 1.

After one year from the ratification of this article the manufacture, sale, or transportation of intoxicating liquors within, the importation thereof into, or the exportation thereof from the United States and all territory subject to the jurisdiction thereof for beverage purposes is hereby prohibited.

Section 2.

The Congress and the several States shall have concurrent power to enforce this article by appropriate legislation.

Section 3.

This article shall be inoperative unless it shall have been ratified as an amendment to the Constitution by the legislatures of the several States, as provided in the Constitution, within seven years from the date of the submission hereof to the States by the Congress.

Amendment XIX

The right of citizens of the United States to vote shall not be denied or abridged by the United States or by any State on account of sex.

Congress shall have power to enforce this article by appropriate legislation.

Amendment XX

Section 1.

The terms of the President and the Vice President shall end at noon on the 20th day of January, and the terms of Senators and Representatives at noon on the 3d day of January, of the years in which such terms would have ended if this article had not been ratified; and the terms of their successors shall then begin.

Section 2.

The Congress shall assemble at least once in every year, and such meeting shall begin at noon on the 3d day of January, unless they shall by law appoint a different day.

Section 3.

If, at the time fixed for the beginning of the term of the President, the President elect shall have died, the Vice President elect shall become President. If a President shall not have been chosen before the time fixed for the beginning of his term, or if the President elect shall have failed to qualify, then the Vice President elect shall act as President until a President shall have qualified; and the Congress may by law provide for the case wherein neither a President elect nor a Vice President elect shall have qualified, declaring who shall then act as President, or the manner in which one who is to act shall be selected, and such person shall act accordingly until a President or Vice President shall have qualified.

Section 4.

The Congress may by law provide for the case of the death of any of the persons from whom the House of Representatives may choose a President whenever the right of choice shall have devolved upon them, and for the case of the death of any of the persons from whom the Senate may choose a Vice President whenever the right of choice shall have devolved upon them.

Section 5.

Sections 1 and 2 shall take effect on the 15th day of October following the ratification of this article.

Section 6.

This article shall be inoperative unless it shall have been ratified as an amendment to the Constitution by the legislatures of three-fourths of the several States within seven years from the date of its submission.

Amendment XXI

Section 1.

The eighteenth article of amendment to the Constitution of the United States is hereby repealed.

Section 2.

The transportation or importation into any State, Territory, or possession of the United States for delivery or use therein of intoxicating liquors, in violation of the laws thereof, is hereby prohibited.

Section 3.

This article shall be inoperative unless it shall have been ratified as an amendment to the Constitution by conventions in the several States, as provided in the Constitution, within seven years from the date of the submission hereof to the States by the Congress.

Amendment XXII

Section 1.

No person shall be elected to the office of the President more than twice, and no person who has held the office of President, or acted as President, for more than two years of a term to which some other person was elected President shall be elected to the office of the President more than once. But this Article shall not apply to any person holding the office of President when this Article was proposed by the Congress, and shall not prevent any person who may be holding the office of President, or acting as President, during the term within which this Article becomes operative from holding the office of President or acting as President during the remainder of such term.

Section 2.

This article shall be inoperative unless it shall have been ratified as an amendment to the Constitution by the legislatures of three-fourths of the several States within seven years from the date of its submission to the States by the Congress.

Amendment XXIII

Section 1.

The District constituting the seat of Government of the United States shall appoint in such manner as the Congress may direct:

A number of electors of President and Vice President equal to the whole number of Senators and Representatives in Congress to which the District would be entitled if it were a State, but in no event more than the least populous State; they shall be in addition to those appointed by the States, but they shall be considered, for the purposes of the election of President and Vice President, to be electors appointed by a State; and they shall meet in the District and perform such duties as provided by the twelfth article of amendment.

Section 2.

The Congress shall have power to enforce this article by appropriate legislation.

Amendment XXIV

Section 1.

The right of citizens of the United States to vote in any primary or other election for President or Vice President, for electors for President or Vice President, or for Senator or Representative in Congress, shall not be denied or abridged by the United States or any State by reason of failure to pay any poll tax or other tax.

Section 2.

The Congress shall have power to enforce this article by appropriate legislation.

Amendment XXV

Section 1.

In case of the removal of the President from office or of his death or resignation, the Vice President shall become President.

Section 2.

Whenever there is a vacancy in the office of the Vice President, the President shall nominate a Vice President who shall take office upon confirmation by a majority vote of both Houses of Congress.

Section 3.

Whenever the President transmits to the President pro tempore of the Senate and the Speaker of the House of Representatives his written declaration that he is unable to discharge the powers and duties of his office, and until he transmits to them a written declaration to the contrary, such powers and duties shall be discharged by the Vice President as Acting President.

Section 4.

Whenever the Vice President and a majority of either the principal officers of the executive departments or of such other body as Congress may by law provide, transmit to the President pro tempore of the Senate and the Speaker of the House of Representatives their written declaration that the President is unable to discharge the powers and duties of his office, the Vice President shall immediately assume the powers and duties of the office as Acting President.

Thereafter, when the President transmits to the President pro tempore of the Senate and the Speaker of the House of Representatives his written declaration that no inability exists, he shall resume the powers and duties of his office unless the Vice President and a majority of either the principal officers of the executive department or of such other body as Congress may by law provide, transmit within four days to the President pro tempore of the Senate and the Speaker of the House of Representatives their written declaration that the President is unable to discharge the powers and duties of his office. Thereupon Congress shall decide the issue, assembling within forty-eight hours for that purpose if not in session. If the Congress, within twenty-one days after receipt of the latter written declaration, or, if Congress is not in session, within twenty-one days after Congress is required to assemble, determines by two-thirds vote of both Houses that the President is unable to discharge the powers and duties of his office, the Vice President shall continue to discharge the same as Acting President; otherwise, the President shall resume the powers and duties of his office.

Amendment XXVI

Section 1.

The right of citizens of the United States, who are eighteen years of age or older, to vote shall not be denied or abridged by the United States or by any State on account of age.

Section 2.

The Congress shall have power to enforce this article by appropriate legislation.

Amendment XXVII

No law, varying the compensation for the services of the Senators and Representatives, shall take effect, until an election of Representatives shall have intervened.

ABOUT THE AUTHOR

Tom McHale is the Director of Public Policy and Digital Media for the American Constitutional Rights Union and ACRU Action Fund.

Tom McHale is an author and Editor of American Handgunner magazine. He's published seven books to date. During the past 10 years, Tom has published nearly 2,000 articles across a variety of publications.

Prior to his writing career, Tom spent 25 years working in the technology industry as a marketing executive and strategic alliances director. From his time immersed in the tech space, Tom understands not only the opportunities possible from the industry, but the potential dangers, pitfalls, and threats to privacy and freedom.

Tom is a graduate of Emory University with a major in Economics and a minor in Computer Science. He completed his Master's Degree in Business Administration at the University of North Florida with a concentration in Finance and Marketing.

tom-mchale.com

facebook.com/tommchaleauthor
twitter.com/tommchale
linkedin.com/in/tomwmchale

ALSO BY TOM MCHALE

The Practical Guide to Guns and Shooting

The Practical Guide to Gun Holsters for Concealed Carry

The Practical Guide to Reloading Ammunition

30 Days to Concealed Carry Confidence

Armed and Ready: Your Comprehensive Blueprint to Concealed Carry
Confidence

Made in United States
Orlando, FL
16 December 2023

41033426R00114